Allyn & Bacon Casebook Series
Foster Care

Edited by

Jerry L. Johnson

Grand Valley State University

George Grant, Jr.

Grand Valley State University

PEARSON

Boston   New York   San Francisco
Mexico City   Montreal   Toronto   London   Madrid   Munich   Paris
Hong Kong   Singapore   Tokyo   Cape Town   Sydney

*To all of those who have helped, advised, supported, criticized,
and forgiven. You know who you are.*
Jerry L. Johnson

*To my wife, Beverly, who inspires and supports me
in all my endeavors. In loving memory of my father and mother,
George and Dorothy Grant, and Daisy Franks.*
George Grant, Jr.

Series Editor: *Patricia Quinlin*
Marketing Manager: *Kris Ellis-Levy*
Production Administrator: *Janet Domingo*
Compositor: *Galley Graphics*
Composition Buyer: *Linda Cox*
Manufacturing Buyer: *JoAnne Sweeney*
Cover Coordinator: *Rebecca Krzyzaniak*

For related titles and support materials, visit our online catalog at www.ablongman.com.

Copyright © 2005 Pearson Education, Inc.

Library of Congress Cataloging-in-Publication Data

Allyn and Bacon casebook series for foster care / [edited by] Jerry L. Johnson, George
    Grant, Jr.
    p. cm.
    Includes bibliographical references.
    ISBN 0-205-38950-3 (pbk.)
    1. Foster home care—United States—Case studies.   2. Family social work—United
    States—Case studies.   I. Johnson, Jerry L.   II. Grant, George, Jr.
    HV881.A627 2005
    362.73′3′0973—dc22

                                                                        2004052962

Printed in the United States of America

10   9   8   7   6   5   4   3   2   1   09   08   07   06   05   04

Contents

Preface

This text offers students the chance to study the work of experienced social workers practicing in foster care settings. As graduate and undergraduate social work educators, we (the editors) have struggled to find quality practice materials that translate well into a classroom setting. Over the years, we have used case materials from our practice careers, professionally produced audio-visuals, and tried other casebooks. While each had its advantages, we could not find a vehicle that allowed students to study the work of experienced practitioners and travel beyond the belief that practice is a technical endeavor that involves finding "correct" interventions to solve client problems.

We want our students to study and analyze how experienced practitioners think about practice and how they struggle to resolve ethical dilemmas and make treatment decisions that meet the needs of their clientele. We want students to review and challenge the work of others in a way that allows them to understand what comprises important practice decisions with real clients in real practice settings. That is, we want classroom materials that allow students entry into the minds of experienced practitioners.

Goals of the Casebook

This Casebook focuses on practice with clients in foster care in a variety of settings and from diverse backgrounds. Our goal is to provide students with an experience that:

1. Provides personal and intimate glimpses into the thinking and actions of experienced practitioners as they work with clients. In each case, students may demonstrate their understanding of the cases and how and/or why the authors approached their case in the manner presented.

2. Provides a vehicle to evaluate the process, ideas, and methods used by the authors. We also wanted to provide students with a chance to present their ideas about how they would have worked differently with the same case.

3. Affords students the opportunity to use evidence-based practice findings (Gibbs, 2003; Cournoyer, 2004) as part of the case review and planning process. We challenge students to base practice judgments and case planning exercises on current practice evidence available through library and/or electronic searches, and to practice wisdom gained through consultation and personal experience when the evidence is conflicted or lacking.

To meet our goals, the cases we included in this text focus on the practice *process,* specifically client engagement, assessment, and the resultant clinical process. The cases explore the inevitable ethical dilemmas that consistently arise in daily practice. We aim to demonstrate the technical and artistic elements involved in developing and managing the various simultaneous processes involved in practice. While we recognize the difficulty of presenting process information (circular) in a linear medium (book), we have tried to do the best job possible toward this end.

To achieve our goals, we include four in-depth case studies in this text. In these case studies, authors guide students through the complete practice process, from initial contact to client termination and practice evaluation. Focusing heavily on multi-systemic client life history (see Chapter 1), students get a detailed look into the life history and presentation of the client. Then, we challenge students to "finish the case" by using client information and classroom learning to develop a written narrative assessment, diagnostic statement, treatment and intervention plan, termination and follow-up plan, and a plan to evaluate practice. We have used these cases as in-class exercises, the basis for semester-long term papers, and as comprehensive final examinations that integrate multifaceted student learning in practice courses across the curriculum.

Rationale

As former practitioners, we chose the cases carefully. Therefore, the cases in this text focus on the process (thinking, planning, and decision-making) of social work practice and not necessarily on techniques or outcome. Do not be fooled by this statement. Obviously, we believe in successful client outcome based, at least in part, on the use of evidence-based practice methods and current research findings. As important as this is, it is not our focus here—with good reason. Our experience suggests that instructive process occurs in cases that have successful and unsuccessful outcome. In fact, we often learned more from unsuccessful cases than successful cases. We learned the most when events did not play out as planned. While some of the cases terminated successfully, others did not. This is not a commentary on the author or the author's skill level. Everyone has cases (sometimes too many) that do not turn out as planned. We chose cases based on one simple criterion: did it provide the best possible hope for practice education? We asked authors to teach practice by considering cases that were interesting and difficult, regardless of outcome. We did not want the Casebook to become simply a vehicle to promote practice brilliance.

Mostly, we wanted this text to differ from other casebooks, because we were unsatisfied with casebooks as teaching tools. As part of the process of planning our Casebooks, we reviewed other casebooks and discussed with our graduate and undergraduate students approaches that best facilitated learning in the classroom. We discovered that many students were also dissatisfied with a casebook approach to education, for a variety of reasons. Below, we briefly address what our students told us about casebooks in general.

1. *Linear presentation.* One of the most significant problems involves case presentation. Generally, this involves two issues: linearity and brevity. Most written case studies give students the impression that practice actually proceeds smoothly, orderly, and sequentially. These cases often leave students believing—or expecting—that clinical decisions are made beforehand and that practice normally proceeds as planned. In other words, students often enter the field believing that casework follows an "*A, leads to B, leads to C, leads to clients living happily ever after*" approach.

Experienced practitioners know better. In over 40 years of combined social work practice in a variety of settings, we have learned—often the "hard way"—that the opposite is true. We rarely, if ever, had a case proceed sequentially, whether our client is an individual, couple, family, group, community, or classroom. That is, the process of engagement (including cultural competence), assessment, treatment planning, intervention, and follow-up occur in a circular manner, rooted in the client's social, physical, and cultural context, and includes consideration of the practitioner, his or her organization, and the laws and policies that affect and/or determine the boundaries of social work practice and treatment funding.

Practice evolves in discontinuous cycles over time, including time-limited treatments mandated by the managed care system. Therefore, real-life clinical practice—just as in all developing human relationships—seems to consistently require stops and starts, take wrong turns, and even, in some cases, require "do-overs." While the goal of competent practice is to facilitate an orderly helping process that includes planned change (Timberlake, Farber, & Sabatino, 2002), practice, as an orderly process, is more often a goal (or a myth) than planned certainty. Given the linearity of case presentations discussed above, readers are often left without an appreciation or understanding of practice as process.

Additionally, many of the case presentation texts we reviewed provided "hard" client data and asked students to develop treatment plans based on this data. Yet, as any experienced practitioner knows, the difficulty in practice occurs during engagement and data collection. The usual case approach often overlooks this important element of practice. While a book format limits process writing, we believe that the case format we devised here brings students closer to the "real thing."

2. *Little focus on client engagement.*   As we like to remind students, there are two words in the title of our profession: social and work. In order for the "work" to be successful, students must learn to master the "social"—primarily client engagement and relationship building. Social work practice is relationship based (Saleebey, 2002) and, from our perspective, relies more on the processes involved in relationship building and client engagement than technical intervention skills (Johnson, 2004). Successful practice is often rooted more in the ability of practitioners to develop open and trusting relationships with client(s) than on their ability to employ specific methods of intervention (Johnson, 2004).

Yet, this critically important element of practice often goes understated or ignored. Some texts even assume that engagement skills somehow exist before learning about practice. We find this true in casebooks and primary practice texts as well. When it is discussed, engagement and relationship building is presented as a technical process that also proceeds in linear fashion. Our experience with students, employees, and practitioner/trainees over the last two decades suggests that it is wrong to assume that students and/or practitioners have competent engagement or relationship building skills. From our perspective, developing a professional relationship that involves trust and openness, where clients feel safe to dialogue about the most intimate and sometimes embarrassing events in their lives, is the primary responsibility of the practitioner. This relationship often spells the difference between positive and negative client outcome (Johnson, 2004; Miller & Rollnick, 2002; Harper & Lantz, 1996). Hence, each case presentation tries to provide a sense of this difficult and often elusive process and some of the ways that the authors overcame challenges to the culturally competent client engagement process.

Target Audience

Our target audience for this text, and the others in the series, are advanced undergraduate as well as foundation and advanced graduate students in social work and other helping disciplines. We have tested our approach with students at several different points in their education. We find that the casebooks can be used as:

- An adjunct learning tool for undergraduates preparing for or already involved in their field practicum.
- Practice education and training for foundation-level graduate students in practice theory and/or methods courses.
- An adjunct learning tool for second-year graduate students in field practicum.
- An adjunct learning tool for undergraduate and/or graduate students in any practice courses pertaining to specific populations.

While we are social work educators, we believe the casebooks will be useful in many disciplines in the human services, including counseling psychology, counseling, mental health, psychology, marriage and family therapy, substance abuse, and mental health degree or certificate programs. Any educational or training program designed to prepare students to work with clients in a helping capacity may find the casebooks useful as a learning tool.

Structure of Cases

We organized the case studies to maximize critical thinking, the use of professional literature, evidenced-based practice knowledge, and classroom discussion in the learning process. At various points throughout each case, we comment on issues and/or dilemmas highlighted by the case. Our comments always end with a series of questions designed to sharpen students' ability to find and evaluate evidence from the professional literature and through classroom discussion. We ask students to collect evidence on different sides of an issue, evaluate that evidence, and develop a professional position that they can defend in writing and/or discussion with other students in the classroom or seminar setting.

We hope that you find the cases and our format as instructive and helpful in your courses as we have in ours. We have field-tested our format in courses at our university, finding that students respond well to the length, depth, and rigor of the case presentations. Universally, students report that the case materials were an important part of their overall learning process.

Organization of the Text

We organized this text to maximize its utility in any course. Chapter 1 provides an overview of the Advanced Multi-Systemic (AMS) practice approach. We provide this as one potential organizing tool for students to use while reading and evaluating the subsequent cases. This chapter offers students an organized and systematic framework to use when analyzing cases and/or formulating narrative assessments, treatment, and intervention plans. Our intent is to provide a helpful tool, not make a political statement about the efficacy or popularity of one practice framework versus others. In fact, we invite faculty and students to apply whatever practice framework they wish when working the cases.

In Chapter 2, *Kathy A. Miller, MSW* presents a case entitled **Crisis and Kinship in Foster Care.** This case involves a single mother unable to provide for her three children and an uncle who denied placement of the children in his home. The case explores the needs of the children, the rights of relatives in foster care placements, and how race and culture can influence decisions and outcomes for children in need of permanency.

In Chapter 3, *George Grant, Jr., Ph.D., MSW* presents his work in **Lost in a Foreign Land.** The case discusses Omar, a seventeen-year-old refugee living in foster care in the United States. The case addressed his journey to the United States, his struggle to adjust to a new environment, how racism threatened to alter his life, and his need for permanency. Grant, Jr., demonstrates a therapeutic technique that incorporates Omar's ability to survive in multiple environments, while illustrating that macro systems must be assessed as part of any assessment tool.

In Chapter 4, *Dianne Green-Smith, MSW* presents a case entitled **The Leon Family.** In this case, Green-Smith presents a family involved in both the legal and medical systems. As a family struggles to maintain custody of their children, they must also fight health problems that could put their children at risk. The author introduces a multi-systemic approach to working with the family. She also demonstrates how a family's past can repeat itself if the family is unable to recognize the patterns.

The final chapter, **Dan,** presents the work of *Brian J. De Vos, MSW* with a young man that spent the majority of his life in the foster care system. De Vos demonstrates the complexities of a man who lived in multiple foster care systems, and in adulthood is still dealing with his foster care experiences. The author also addresses the ethical issue of under what circumstances should a therapist take or transfer a case.

Acknowledgments

We would like to thank the contributors to this text, Kathy A. Miller, Dianne Green-Smith, and Brian J. De Vos, for their willingness to allow their work to be challenged and discussed in a public venue. We would also like to thank Patricia Quinlin and her people at Allyn and Bacon for their faith in the Casebook Series and in our ability to manage fourteen manuscripts at once. Additionally, we have to thank all of our students and student assistants that served as "guinea pigs" for our case studies. Their willingness to provide honest feedback contributes mightily to this series.

Jerry L. Johnson—I want to thank my wife, Cheryl, for her support and willingness to give me the time and encouragement to write and edit. I also owe a debt of gratitude to my dear friend Hope, for being there when I need you the most.

George Grant, Jr.—I want to thank Dean Rodney Mulder, Dr. Elaine Schott, Dr. Doris Perry, and Professor Emily Jean McFadden for their insight, encouragement, and support during this process. To Lisa Neimeyer and Kimberly S. Crawford for their eye for detail. Finally, I want to thank Alice D. Denton and Alyson D. Grant for their continued support and Dr. Julius Franks and Professor Daniel Groce for their intellectual discourse and unwavering support.

Contributors

The Editors

Jerry L. Johnson, Ph.D., MSW is an Associate Professor in the School of Social Work at Grand Valley State University in Grand Rapids, Michigan. He received his MSW from Grand Valley State University and his Ph.D. in sociology from Western

Michigan University. Johnson has been in social work for more than 20 years as a practitioner, supervisor, administrator, consultant, teacher, and trainer. He was the recipient of two Fulbright Scholarship awards to Albania in 1998–99 and 2000–01. In addition to teaching and writing, Johnson serves in various consulting capacities in countries such as Albania and Armenia. He is the author of two previous books, *Crossing Borders—Confronting History: Intercultural Adjustment in a Post-Cold War World* (2000, Rowan and Littlefield) and *Fundamentals of Substance Abuse Practice* (2004, Wadsworth Brooks/Cole).

George Grant, Jr., Ph.D., MSW is an Associate Professor in the School of Social Work at Grand Valley State University in Grand Rapids, Michigan. Grant, Jr., also serves as the Director of Grand Valley State University's MSW Program. He received his MSW from Grand Valley State University and Ph.D. in sociology from Western Michigan University. Grant, Jr., has a long and distinguished career as practitioner, administrator, consultant, teacher, and trainer in social work, primarily in fields dedicated to Child Welfare.

Contributors

Kathy A. Miller, MSW is a Services Program Manager/Child Welfare Supervisor for a county Family Independence Agency. Her duties include working as a first line supervisor in the children's foster care, adoption, foster home certification, and guardianship programs. Miller provides secondary supervision to the children's protective services, juvenile justice, prevention, and adult services. She has worked on numerous community and administrative projects, addressing issues of policy, funding, and collaboration. Miller has a MSW from Grand Valley State University and a BA in Psychology from the University of Michigan.

Dianne Green-Smith, MSW, CSW, ACSW, LCSW is an Assistant Professor in the School of Social Work at Grand Valley State University in Grand Rapids, Michigan. She has a BA from Xavier University, an MSW from Tulane University, and is currently completing her Ph.D. in social work from Loyola University. Green-Smith has over 25 years of practice experience, specializing in work with families and children, couples therapy, parenting groups, pregnancy and infant adoption, and HIV/AIDS. She is active in community events and public service.

Brian J. De Vos, MSW is Director of Operations at Bethany Christian Services. De Vos oversees all of the child welfare programs for Bethany in the state of Michigan. The services include foster, contact adoption, family counseling, infant adoption, pregnancy counseling, volunteer services and family preservation programs. He has over 19 years of practice experience in residential, foster care, and mental health, and he was the children's Ombudsman for a county mental health system. De Vos received his BA from Calvin and an MSW from Grand Valley State University.

Bibliography

Cournoyer, B. R. (2004). *The evidence-based social work skills book.* Boston: Allyn and Bacon.

Gibbs, L. E. (2003). *Evidence-based practice for the helping professions: A practical guide with integrated multimedia.* Pacific Grove, CA: Brooks/Cole.

Harper, K. V., & Lantz, J. (1996). *Cross-cultural practice: Social work practice with diverse populations.* Chicago: Lyceum Books.

Johnson, J. L. (2004). *Fundamentals of substance abuse practice.* Pacific Grove, CA: Brooks/Cole.

Miller, W. R., & Rollnick, S. (2002). *Motivational interviewing: Preparing people to change addictive behavior* (2nd ed.). New York: Guilford Press.

Saleebey, D. (2002). *The strengths perspective in social work practice* (3rd ed.). Boston: Allyn and Bacon.

Timberlake, E. M., Farber, M. Z., & Sabatino, C. A. (2002). *The general method of social work practice: McMahon's generalist perspective* (4th ed.). Boston: Allyn and Bacon.

A Multi-Systemic Approach to Practice

Jerry L. Johnson & George Grant, Jr.

This is a practice-oriented text, designed to build practice skills with individuals, families, and groups. We intend to provide you with the opportunity to study the process involved in treating real cases from the caseloads of experienced practitioners. Unlike other casebooks, we include fewer cases, but provide substantially more detail in hopes of providing a realistic look into the thinking, planning, and approach of the practitioners/authors. We challenge you to study the authors' thinking and methods to understand their approach and then use critical thinking skills and your own knowledge to propose alternative ways of treating the same clients. In other words, what would your course of action be if you were the primary practitioner responsible for these cases? Our hope is that this text provides a worthwhile and rigorous experience studying real cases as they progressed in practice.

Before proceeding to the cases, we include this chapter as an introduction to the Advanced Multi-Systemic (AMS) practice perspective. We decided to present this introduction with two primary goals in mind. First, we want you to use the information contained in this chapter to help assess and analyze the cases in this text. You will have the opportunity to complete a multi-systemic assessment, diagnoses, treatment, and intervention plan for each case. This chapter will provide the theoretical and practical basis for this exercise. Second, we hope you find that AMS makes conceptualizing cases clearer in your practice environment. We do not suggest that AMS is the only way, or even the best way for every practitioner to conceptualize cases. We simply know, through experience, that AMS is an effective way to think about practice with client-systems of all sizes and configurations. While there are many approaches to practice, AMS offers an effective way to place clinical decisions in the context of client lives and experiences, making engagement and treatment productive for clients and practitioners.

Advanced Multi-Systemic (AMS) Practice

Sociological Roots

> Whether the point of interest is a great power state or a minor literary mood, a family, a prison, and a creed—these are the kinds of questions the best social analysts have asked. They are the intellectual pivots of classic studies of (person) in society—and they are the questions inevitably raised by any mind possessing the sociological imagination. For that imagination is the capacity to shift from one perspective to another— from the political to the psychological; from examination of a single family to comparative assessment of the national budgets of the world; from the theological school to the military establishment; from considerations of an oil industry to studies of contemporary poetry. It is the capacity to range from the most impersonal and remote transformations to the most intimate features of the human self—and see the relations between the two. Back of its use is always the urge to know the social and historical meaning of the individual in the society and in the period in which he (or she) has his quality and his (or her) being. (Mills, 1959, p. 7; parentheses added)

Above, sociologist C. Wright Mills provided a seminal description of the sociological imagination. As it turns out, Mills's sociological imagination is also an apt description of AMS. Mills believed that linking people's "private troubles" to "public issues" (p. 2) was the most effective way to understand people and their issues, by placing them in historical context. It forces investigators to contextualize individuals, families, and communities in the framework of the larger social, political, economic, and historical environments in which they live. Ironically, this is also the goal of social work practice (Germain & Gitterman, 1996; Longres, 2000). Going further, Mills (1959) stated:

> We have come to know that every individual lives, from one generation to the next, in some society; that he (or she) lives out a biography, and that he (or she) lives it out within some historical sequence. By the fact of his (or her) living he (or she) contributes, however minutely, to the shaping of this society and to the course of its history, even as he (or she) is made by society and by its historical push and shove. (p. 6)

Again, Mills was not speaking as a social worker. He was an influential sociologist, speaking about a method of social research. In *The Sociological Imagination,* Mills (1959) proposed this as a method to understand the links between people, their daily lives, and their multi-systemic environment. Yet, while laying the theoretical groundwork for social research, Mills also provided the theoretical foundation for an effective approach to social work practice. We find four relevant points in *The Sociological Imagination* that translate directly to social work practice.

1. It is crucial to recognize the relationships between people's personal issues and strengths (private troubles) and the issues (political, economic, social, historical, and legal) and strengths of the multi-systemic environment (public issues) in which people live daily and across their life span. A multi-systemic understanding includes recognizing and integrating issues and strengths at the micro (individual, family, extended kin, etc.), mezzo (local community), and macro (state, region, national, and international policy, laws, political, economic, and social) levels during client engagement, assessment, treatment, follow-up, and evaluation of practice. This is true whether your client is an individual, family, small group, or community association. This requirement does not change, only the point where investigation begins.

2. This depth of understanding (by social workers and, especially, clients) can lead to change in people's lives. We speak here about second-order change, or, significant change that makes a long-term difference in people's lives; change that helps people view themselves differently in relationship to their world. This level of change becomes possible when people, alone or in groups, make multi-systemic links in a way that makes sense to them (Freire, 1993). In other words, clients become "empowered" to change when they understand their life in the context of their world and realize that they have previously unforeseen or unimagined choices in how they live, think, believe, and act.

3. Any assessment and/or clinical diagnoses that exclude multi-systemic links do not provide a holistic picture of people's lives, their troubles, and/or strengths. In sociology, this leads to a reductionist view of people and society, while in social work it reduces the likelihood that services will be provided (or received by clients) in a way that addresses client problems and utilizes client strengths in a meaningful way. The opportunity for change is reduced whenever client life history is overlooked because it does not fit, or is not called for, in a practitioner's preferred method of helping, or because of shortcuts many people believe are needed in a managed care environment. One cannot learn too much about their clients, their lives, and their attitudes, beliefs, and values as it relates to the private troubles presented in treatment.

4. Inherent in AMS and foundational to achieving all that was discussed above relies on practitioners being able to rapidly develop rapport with clients and client systems that leads to engagement in treatment or action. In this text, client engagement

> . . . occurs when you develop, in collaboration with clients, a trusting and open professional relationship that promotes hope and presents viable prospects for change. Successful engagement occurs when you create a social context in which vulnerable people (who often hold jaded attitudes toward helping professionals) can share their innermost feelings, as well as their most embarrassing and shameful behavior with you, a *total stranger.* (Johnson, 2004, p. 93; emphasis in original)

AMS Overview

First, we should define two important terms that comprise AMS. Understanding these terms is important, because they provide the foundation for understanding the language and concepts used throughout the remainder of this chapter.

1. Advanced.   According to Derezotes (2000), "the most advanced theory is also the most inclusive" (p. viii). AMS is advanced because it is inclusive. It requires responsible practitioners in positions of responsibility (perhaps as solo practitioners) to acquire a depth of knowledge, skills, and self-awareness. This allows for an inclusive application of knowledge acquired in the areas of human behavior in the social environment, social welfare policy, social research and practice evaluation, and multiple practice methods and approaches in service of clients and client systems of various sizes, types, and configurations.

AMS practitioners are expected to have the most inclusive preparation possible, "both the broad generalist base of knowledge, skills, and values and an in-depth proficiency in practice . . . with selected social work methods and populations" (Derezotes, 2000, p. xii). Hence, advanced practitioners are well trained and, with in-depth knowledge, are often in positions of being responsible for clients as primary practitioners. They are afforded the responsibility for engaging, assessing, intervening, and evaluating practice, ensuring that clients are ethically treated in a way that is culturally competent and respectful of their client's worldview. In other words, AMS practitioners develop the knowledge, skills, and values needed to be leaders in their organizations, communities, the social work profession, and especially in the treatment of their clients. The remainder of this chapter explains why AMS is an advanced approach to practice.

2. Multi-Systemic.   From the earliest moments in their education, social workers learn a systems perspective that emphasizes the connectedness between people and their problems to the complex interrelationships that exist in their client's world (Timberlake, Farber, & Sabatino, 2002). To explain these connections, systems theory emphasizes three important concepts: wholeness, relationships, and homeostasis. Wholeness refers to the notion that the various parts or elements (subsystem) of a system interact to form a whole that best describes the system in question. This concept asserts that no system can be understood or explained unless the connectedness of the subsystems to the whole is understood or explained. In other words, the whole is greater than the sum of its parts. Moreover, systems theory also posits that change in one subsystem will affect change in the system as a whole.

In terms of systems theory, relationship refers to the patterns of interaction and overall structures that exist within and between subsystems. The nature of these relationships is more important than the system itself. That is, when trying to understand or explain a system (individual, family, or organization, etc.), we should look at how subsystems connect through relationships, the characteristics of the relationships between subsystems, and how the subsystems interact to provide clues to understanding the system as a whole. Hence, the application of systems theory is primarily based on understanding relationships. As someone once said about systems theory, in systems problems occur between people and subsystems (relationships), not "in" them. People's internal problems relate to the nature of the relationships in the systems where they live and interact.

Homeostasis refers to the notion that most living systems work to maintain and preserve the existing system, or the status quo. For example, family members often assume roles that serve to protect and maintain family stability, often at the expense of "needed" change. The same can be said for organizations, groups, or community associations. The natural tendency toward homeostasis in systems represents what we call the "dilemma of change" (Johnson, 2004). This can best be described as the apparent conflict, or what appears to be client resistance or lack of motivation, that often occurs when clients approach moments of significant change. Systems of all types and configurations struggle with the dilemma of change: should they change to the unknown or remain the same, even if the status quo is unhealthy or unproductive? Put differently, systems strive for stability, even at the expense of health and well being of individual members and/or the system itself.

What do we mean, then, by the term *multi-systemic*? Clients (individuals, families, communities, etc.) are systems that interact with a number of different systems simultaneously. These systems exist and interact at multiple levels, ranging from the micro level (individual and families), the mezzo level (local community, institutions, organizations, the practitioner and their agency, etc.), to the macro level (culture, laws and policy, politics, oppression and discrimination, international events, etc.). How these various systems come together, interact, and adapt, along with the relationships that exist within and between each system, work together to comprise the "whole" that is the client, or client-system.

In practice, the client (individual, couple, family, community, etc.) is not the "system," but one of many interacting subsystems in a maze of other subsystems constantly interacting to create the system—the client plus elements from multiple subsystems at each level. It would be a mistake to view the client as the whole system. They are but one facet of a multidimensional and multi-level system comprised of the client and various other subsystems at the micro, mezzo, and macro levels.

Therefore, the term *multi-systemic* refers to the nature of a system comprised of the various multi-level subsystems described above. A multi-systemic perspective recognizes that clients or client systems are *one part or subsystem* in relationship with other subsystemic influences occurring on different levels. This level of understanding—the system as the whole produced through multi-systemic subsystem interactions—is the main unit of investigation for practice. As stated above, it is narrow to consider the client as a functioning independent system with peripheral involvement with other systems existing outside of his or her intimate world. These issues and relationships work together to help shape and mold the client who, in turn, shapes and molds his or her relationship to the other subsystems. Yet, the person-of-the-client is but one part of the system in question during practice.

AMS provides an organized framework for gathering, conceptualizing, and analyzing multi-systemic client data and for proceeding with the helping process. It defines the difference between social work and other disciplines in the helping pro-

fessions at the level of theory and practice. How, you ask? Unlike other professional disciplines that tend to focus on one or a few domains (i.e., psychology, medicine,
etc.), AMS provides a comprehensive and holistic "picture" of clients or client-systems in the context of their environment by considering information about multiple
personal and systemic domains simultaneously. Moreover, practitioners can use
AMS to address clients and client systems of all sizes and configurations. That is,
this approach works as well with communities or international projects as it does
with individuals or families seeking therapy.

Resting on the generalist foundation taught in all Council on Social Work
Education (CSWE) accredited undergraduate and foundation-level graduate programs, AMS requires practitioners to contextualize client issues in the context of the
multiple interactions that occur between the client/client-system and the social, economic, legal, political, and physical environment in which the client lives. It is a unifying perspective based in the client's life, history, and culture that guides the
process of collecting and analyzing client life information and intervening to promote personal choice through a comprehensive, multi-systemic framework.
Beginning with culturally competent client engagement, a comprehensive multi-
systemic assessment points toward a holistically based treatment plan that requires
practitioners to select and utilize appropriate practice theories, models, and methods—or combinations thereof—that best fit the client's unique circumstances and
needs.

AMS is not a practice theory, model, or method itself. It is a perspective or
framework for conceptualizing client-systems. It relies on the practitioner's ability
to use a variety of theories, models, and methods, and to incorporate knowledge
from human behavior, social policy, research/evaluation, and practice into his or her
routine approach with clients. For example, AMS practitioners will have the skills
to apply different approaches to individual treatment (client-centered, cognitive-
behavioral, etc.), family treatment (structural, narrative, Bowenian, etc.), couples,
and groups; they could arrange for specialized care if needed, and act as an advocate on behalf of their client. AMS may also require practitioners to treat clients in
a multi-modal approach (i.e., individual and group treatments simultaneously).
Additionally, AMS practitioners can work with community groups and organizations at the local, regional, or national level.

Practitioners not only must know how to apply different approaches but also
how to determine, primarily through the early engagement and assessment process,
which theory, model, or approach (direct or indirect, for example) would work best
for a particular client. Hence, successful practice using AMS relies heavily on the
practitioner's ability to competently engage and multi-systemically assess client
problems and strengths. Practitioners must simultaneously develop a sense of their
client's personal interaction and relationship style—especially related to how they
relate to authority figures—when determining which approach would best suit the
client. For example, a reserved, quiet, or thoughtful client or someone who lacks
assertiveness may not be well served by a directive, confrontational approach,
regardless of the practitioner's preference. Moreover, AMS practitioners rely on
professional practice research and outcome studies to help determine which

approach or intervention package might work best for particular clients and/or client systems. AMS expects practitioners to know how to find and evaluate practice research in their practice areas or specialties.

Elements of the Advanced Multi-Systemic Approach to Social Work Practice

The advanced multi-systemic approach entails the following seven distinct, yet integrated elements of theory and practice. Each is explained below.

Ecological Systems Perspective

One important subcategory of systems therapy for social work is the ecological systems perspective. This perspective combines important concepts from the science of ecology and general systems theory into a way of viewing client problems and strengths in social work practice. In recent years, it has become the prevailing perspective for social work practice (Miley, O'Melia, & DuBois, 2004). The ecological systems perspective—sometimes referred to as the ecosystems perspective—is a useful metaphor for guiding social workers as they think about cases (Germain & Gitterman, 1980).

Ecology focuses on how subsystems work together and adapt. In ecology, adaptation is "a dynamic process between people and their environments as people grow, achieve competence, and make contributions to others" (Greif, 1986, p. 225). Insight from ecology leads to an analysis of how people fit within their environment and what adaptations are made in the fit between people and their environments. Problems develop as a function of inadequate or improper adaptation or fit between people and their environments.

General systems theory focuses on how human systems interact. It focuses specifically on how people grow, survive, change, and achieve stability or instability in the complex world of multiple systemic interactions (Miley, O'Melia, & DuBois, 2004). General systems theory has contributed significantly to the growth of the family therapy field and to how social workers understand their clients.

Together, ecology and general systems theory evolved into what social workers know as the ecological systems perspective. The ecological systems perspective provides a systemic framework for understanding the many ways that persons and environments interact. Accordingly, individuals and their individual circumstances can be understood in the context of these interactions. The ecological systems perspective provides an important part of the foundation for AMS. Miley, O'Melia, and DuBois (2004) provide an excellent summary of the ecological systems perspective. They suggest that it

1. Presents a dynamic view of human beings as system interactions in context.
2. Emphasizes the significance of human system interactions.

3. Traces how human behavior and interaction develop over time in response to internal and external forces.
4. Describes current behavior as an adaptive fit of "persons in situations."
5. Conceptualizes all interaction as adaptive or logical in context.
6. Reveals multiple options for change within persons, their social groups, and in their social and physical environments (p. 33).

Social Constructionism

To maintain AMS as an inclusive practice approach, we need to build on the ecological systems perspective by including ideas derived from social constructionism. Social constructionism builds on the ecological systems perspective by introducing ideas about how people define themselves and their environment. Social constructionism also, by definition, introduces the role of culture in the meaning people give to themselves and other systems in their multi-systemic environments. The ecological systems perspective discusses relationships at the systemic level. Social constructionism introduces meaning and value into the equation, allowing for a deeper understanding and appreciation of the nature of multi-systemic relationships and adaptations.

Usually, people assume that reality is something "out there" that hits them in the face, something that independently exists, and people must learn to "deal with it." Social constructionism posits something different. Evolving as a critique of the "one reality" belief system, social constructionism points out that the world is comprised of multiple realities. People define their own reality and then live within those definitions. Accordingly, the definition of reality will be different for everyone. Hence, social constructionism deals primarily with meaning, or the systemic processes by which people come to define themselves in their social world. As sociologist W. I. Thomas said, in what has become known as the Thomas Theorem, "If people define situations as real, they are real in their consequences."

For example, some people believe that they can influence the way computerized slot machines pay out winnings by the way they sit, the feeling they get from the machine as they look at it in the casino, by the clothes they are wearing, or by how they trigger the machine, either by pushing the button or pulling the handle. Likewise, many athletes believe that a particular article of clothing, a routine for getting dressed, and/or a certain pregame meal dictates the quality of their athletic prowess that day.

Illogical to most people, the belief that they can influence a computerized machine, that the machine emits feelings, or that an article of clothing dictates athletic prowess is real to some people. For these people, their beliefs influence the way they live. Perhaps you have ideas or "superstitions" that you believe influence how your life goes on a particular day. This is a common occurrence. These people are not necessarily out of touch with objective reality. While people may know, at some level, that slot machines pay according to preset, computerized odds or that athletic prowess has nothing to do with dressing routines, the belief systems continue. What dictates the behavior and beliefs discussed above or in daily "superstitutions" have nothing to do with objective reality and everything to do with people's subjective reality. Subjective reality—or a person's learned definition of the situation—overrides objectivity and helps determine how people behave and/or what they believe.

While these examples may be simplistic, according to social constructionism, the same processes influence everyone—always. In practice, understanding that people's behavior does not depend on the objective existence of something, but on their subjective interpretation of it, is crucial to effective application of AMS. This knowledge is most helpful during client engagement. If practitioners remember that practice is about understanding people's perceptions and not objective reality, they reduce the likelihood that clients will feel misunderstood, there will be fewer disagreements, and it becomes easier to avoid the trap of defining normal behavior as client resistance or a diagnosable mental disorder. This perspective contributes to a professional relationship based in the client's life and belief systems, is consistent with his or her worldview, and one that is culturally appropriate for the client. Being mindful that the definitions people learn from their culture underlies not only what they do but also what they perceive, feel, and think places practitioners on the correct path to "start where the client is." Social constructionism emphasizes the cultural uniqueness of each client and/or client-system and the need to understand each client and/or client-system in her own context and belief systems, not the practitioner's context or belief systems.

Social constructionism also posits that different people attribute different meaning to the same events, because the interactional contexts and the way individuals interpret these contexts are different for everyone, even within the same family or community. One cannot assume that people raised in the same family will define their social world similarly. Individuals, in the context of their environments, derive meaning through a complex process of individual interpretation. This is how siblings from the same family can be so different, almost as if they did not grow up in the same family. For example, the sound of gunfire in the middle of the night may be frightening or normal, depending upon where a person resides and what is routine and accepted in his specific environment. Moreover, simply because some members of a family or community understand nightly gunfire as normal does not mean that others in the same family or community will feel the same.

Additionally, social constructionism examines how people construct meaning with language and established or evolving cultural beliefs. For example, alcohol consumption is defined as problematic depending upon how the concept of "alcohol problem" is socially constructed in specific environments. Clients from so-called drinking cultures may define drinking six alcoholic drinks daily as normal, while someone from a different cultural background may see this level of consumption as problematic. One of the authors worked in Russia and found an issue that demonstrates this point explicitly. Colleagues in Russia stated rather emphatically that consuming one "bottle" (approximately a U.S. pint) of vodka per day was acceptable and normal. People that consume more than one bottle per day were defined as having a drinking problem. The same level of consumption in the United States would be considered by most as clear evidence of problem drinking.

Biopsychosocial Perspective

Alone, the ecological systems perspective, even with the addition of social constructionism, does not provide the basis for the holistic understanding required by AMS. While it provides a multi-systemic lens, the ecological systems perspective focuses mostly on externals—that is, how people interact and adapt to their environments and how environments interact and adapt to people. Yet, much of what practitioners consider "clinical" focuses on "internals" or human psychological and emotional functioning. Therefore, the ecological systems perspective provides only one part of the holistic picture required by the advanced multi-systemic approach. By adding the biopsychosocial perspective, practitioners can consider the internal workings of human beings to help explain how external and internal subsystems interact.

What is the biopsychosocial perspective? It is a theoretical perspective that considers how human biological, psychological, and social-functioning subsystems interact to account for how people live in their environment. Similar to social systems, human beings are also multidimensional systems comprised of multiple subsystems constantly interacting in their environment, the human body. The biopsychosocial perspective applies multi-systemic thinking to individual human beings.

Several elements comprise the biopsychosocial perspective. Longres (2000) identifies two dimensions of individual functioning, the biophysical, and the psychological. He subdivides the psychological into three subdimensions: the cognitive, affective, and behavioral. Elsewhere, we added the spiritual/existential dimension to this conception (Johnson, 2004). Understanding how the biological, psychological, spiritual and existential, and social subsystems interact is instrumental in developing an appreciation of how individuals influence and are influenced by their social systemic environments. Realizing that each of these dimensions interacts with external social and environmental systems allow practitioners to enlarge their frame of reference, leading to a more holistic multi-systemic view of clients and client-systems.

Strengths/Empowerment Perspective

Over the last few years, the strengths perspective has emerged as an important part of social work theory and practice. The strengths perspective represents a significant change in how social workers conceptualize clients and client-systems. According to Saleebey (2002), it is "a versatile practice approach, relying heavily on ingenuity and creativity . . . Rather than focusing on problems, your eye turns toward possibility" (p. 1). Strengths-based practitioners believe in the power of possibility and hope in helping people overcome problems by focusing on, locating, and supporting existing personal or systemic strengths and resiliencies. The strengths perspective is based on the belief that people, regardless of the severity of their problems, have the capabilities and resources to play an active role in helping solve their own problems. The practitioner's role is to engage clients in a way that unleashes these capabilities and resources toward solving problems and changing lives.

Empowerment

Any discussion of strengths-based approaches must also consider empowerment as an instrumental element of the approach. Empowerment, as a term in social work, has evolved over the years. We choose a definition of empowerment that focuses on power; internal, interpersonal, and environmental (Parsons, Gutierrez, & Cox, 1998). According to Parsons, Gutierrez, and Cox (1998),

> In its most positive sense, power is (1) the ability to influence the course of one's life, (2) an expression of self worth, (3) the capacity to work with others to control aspects of public life, and (4) access to the mechanisms of public decision making. When used negatively, though, it can also block opportunities for stigmatized groups, exclude others and their concerns from decision-making, and be a way to control others. (p. 8)

Hence, empowerment in practice is a process (Parsons, Gutierrez, & Cox, 1998) firmly grounded in ecological systems and strength-based approaches that focus on gaining power by individuals, families, groups, organizations, or communities. It is based on two related assumptions: (1) all human beings are potentially competent, even in extremely challenging situations, and (2) all human beings are subject to various degrees of powerlessness (Cox & Parsons, 1994, p. 17) and oppression (Freire, 1993). People internalize their sense of powerlessness and oppression in a way that their definition of self in the world is limited, often eliminating any notion that they can act in their own behalf in a positive manner.

An empowerment approach makes practical connections between power and powerlessness. It illuminates how these factors interact to influence clients in their daily life. Empowerment is not achieved through a single intervention, nor is it something that can be "done" to another. Empowerment does not occur through neglect or by simply giving responsibility for life and well-being to the poor or troubled, allowing them to be "free" from government regulation, support, or professional assistance. In other words, empowerment of disenfranchised groups does not occur simply by dismantling systems (such as the welfare system) to allow these groups or individuals to take responsibility for themselves. Hence, empowerment does not preclude helping.

Consistent with our definition, empowerment develops through the approach taken toward helping, not the act of helping itself. Empowerment is a sense of gained or regained power that someone attains in his or her life that provides the foundation for change in the short term, and stimulates belief in his or her ability to positively influence his or her life over the long term. Empowerment occurs as a function of the long-term approach of the practitioner and the professional relationship developed between practitioner and client. One cannot provide an empowering context through a constant focus on problems, deficits, inadequacies, negative labeling, and dependency.

The Power of Choice

Choice is an instrumental part of strengths-based and empowerment approaches. We recognize that people, because of inherent strengths and capabilities, can make informed choices about their lives, whether or not they are clients. Practitioners work toward offering people choices about how they define their lives and problems, the extent to which they want to address their problems, and the means or mechanisms through which change should occur. Clients become active and instrumental partners in the helping process. They are not passive vessels, waiting for practitioners to "change them" through some crafty intervention or technique.

We are not talking about the false choices sometimes given to clients by practitioners. For example, clients with substance abuse problems are often told that they must either abstain or leave treatment. Most practitioners ignore, or use as evidence of denial, client requests to attempt so-called controlled use. If practitioners were interested in offering true choice, they would work with these clients toward their controlled-drinking goal in an effort to reduce the potential harm that may result from their use of substances (Johnson, 2004; van Wormer & Davis, 2003), even if the practitioner believes that controlled drinking is not possible. Abstinence would become the goal only when their clients choose to include it as a goal.

Client Engagement as Cultural Competence

Empowerment (choice) occurs through a process of culturally competent client engagement created by identifying strengths, generating dialogue targeted at revealing the extent of people's oppression (Freire, 1993), and respecting their right to make informed choices in their lives. Accordingly, empowerment is the "transformation from individual and collective powerlessness to personal, political, and cultural power" (GlenMaye, 1998, p. 29) through a strengths-based relationship with a professional helper.

Successful application of AMS requires the ability to engage clients in open and trusting professional relationships. The skills needed to engage clients from different backgrounds and with different personal and cultural histories are what drive practice and are what determine the difference between successful and unsuccessful practice. Advanced client engagement skills allow the practitioner to elicit in-depth, multi-systemic information in a dialogue between client and practitioner (Johnson, 2004), providing the foundation for strengths-based client empowerment leading to change.

Earlier, we defined client engagement as a mutual process occurring between clients and practitioners in a professional context created by practitioners. In other words, creating the professional space and open atmosphere that allows engagement to flourish is the primary responsibility of the practitioner, not the client. Practitioners must have the skills and knowledge to adjust their approach toward specific clients and the client's cultural context and not *vice versa*. Clients do not adjust to us and our beliefs, values, and practices—we adjust to them. When that occurs, the foundation exists for client engagement. By definition, relationships of this nature must be performed in a culturally competent manner. Yet, what does this mean?

Over the last two decades, social work and other helping professions have been concerned with cultural competence in practice (Fong, 2001). Beginning in the late 1970s the professional literature has been replete with ideas, definitions, and practice models designed to increase cultural awareness and promote culturally appropriate practice methods. Yet, despite the attention given to the issue, there remains confusion about how to define and teach culturally competent practice.

Structural and Historical Systems of Oppression: Who Holds the Power?

Often embedded in laws, policies, and social institutions are oppressive influences such as racism, sexism, homophobia, and classism. These structural issues play a significant role in the lives of clients (through maltreatment and discrimination) and in social work practice. How people are treated (or how they internalize historical treatment of self, family, friends, and/or ancestors) shapes how they believe, think, and act in the present. Oppression affects how they perceive that others feel about them, how they view the world and their place in it, and how receptive they are to professional service providers. Therefore, culturally competent practice must consider the impact of structural systems of oppression and injustice on clients, their problems, strengths, and potential for change.

Oppression is a by-product of socially constructed notions of power, privilege, control, and hierarchies of difference. As stated above, it is created and maintained by differences in power. By definition, those who have power can force people to abide by the rules, standards, and actions the powerful deem worthwhile, mandatory, or acceptable. Those who hold power can enforce particular worldviews; deny equal access and opportunity to housing, employment, or health care; define right and wrong, normal and abnormal; and imprison, confine, and/or commit physical, emotional, or mental violence against the powerless (McLaren, 1995; Freire, 1993). Most importantly, power permits the holder to "set the very terms of power" (Appleby, 2001, p. 37). It defines the interaction between the oppressed and the oppressor, and between the social worker and client.

Social institutions and practices are developed and maintained by the dominant culture to meet *its* needs and maintain *its* power. Everything and everybody is judged and classified accordingly. Even when the majority culture develops programs or engages in helping activities, these efforts will not include measures that threaten the dominant group's position at the top of the social hierarchy (Freire, 1993). For example, Kozol (1991) wrote eloquently about how public schools fail by design, while Freire (1993) wrote about how state welfare and private charity provide short-term assistance while ensuring that there are not enough resources to lift people permanently out of poverty.

Oppression is neither an academic nor a theoretical consideration; it is not a faded relic of a bygone era. Racism did not end with the civil rights movement, and sexism was not eradicated by the feminist movement. Understanding how systems of oppression work in people's lives is of paramount importance for every individual and family seeking professional help, including those who belong to the *same* race, gender, and class as the practitioner. No two individuals, regardless of their personal demographics, experience the world in the same way. Often, clients are treated ineffectively by professional helpers who mistakenly believe that people who look or act the same will experience the world in similar ways. These workers base their assumptions about clients on stereotypic descriptions of culture, lifestyle, beliefs, and practices. They take group-level data (i.e., many African American adolescents join gangs because of broken families and poverty) and assume that *all* African American teenagers are gang members from single-parent families. Social work values and ethics demand a higher standard, one that compels us to go beyond stereotypes. Our job is to discover, understand, and utilize personal differences in the assessment and treatment process to benefit clients, not use differences as a way of limiting clients' potential for health and well-being.

We cannot accurately assess or treat people without considering the effects of oppression related to race, ethnicity, culture, sexual preference, gender, or physical/emotional status. We need to understand how oppression influences our clients' beliefs about problems and potential approaches to problem solving, and how it determines what kind of support they can expect to receive if they decide to seek help. For example, despite the widely held belief that chemical dependency is an equal opportunity disease (Gordon, 1993), it is clear that some people are more vulnerable than others. While some of the general themes of chemical dependency may appear universal, each client is unique. That is, an individual's dependency results from personal behavior, culture (including the history of one's culture), past experiences, and family interacting with larger social systems that provide opportunities or impose limits on the individual (Johnson, 2000).

Systems of oppression ensure unequal access to resources for certain individuals, families, and communities. However, while all oppressed people are similar in that they lack the power to define their place in the social hierarchy, oppression based on race, gender, sexual orientation, class, and other social factors is expressed in a variety of ways. Learning about cultural nuances is important in client assessment, treatment planning, and treatment (Lum, 1999). According to Pinderhughes (1989), there is no such thing as culture-free service delivery. Cultural differences between clients and social workers in terms of values, norms, beliefs, attitudes, lifestyles, and life opportunities affect every aspect of practice.

What Is Culture?

Many different concepts of culture are used in social work, sociology, and anthropology. Smelser (1992) considers culture a "system of patterned values, meanings, and beliefs that give cognitive structure to the world, provide a basis for coordinating and controlling human interactions, and constitute a link as the system is transmitted from one generation to another" (p. 11). Geertz (1973) regarded culture as simultaneously a product of and a guide to people searching for organized categories and interpretations that provide a meaningful experiential link to their social life. Building upon these two ideas, in this book we abide by the following definition of culture proposed elsewhere (Johnson, 2000):

> Culture is historical, bound up in traditions and practices passed through generations; memories of events—real or imagined—that define a people and their worldview. (Culture) is viewed as collective subjectivity, or a way of life adopted by a community that ultimately defines their worldview. (p. 121)

Consistent with this definition, the collective subjectivities called culture are pervasive forces in the way people interact, believe, think, feel, and act in their social world. Culture plays a significant role in shaping how people view the world. As a historical force, in part built on ideas, definitions, and events passed through generations, culture also defines people's level of social acceptance by the wider community. It shapes how people live, think, and act, and culture influences how people perceive that others feel about them and how they view the world and their place in it. Thus, it is impossible to understand a client without grasping his or her cultural foundations.

Cultural Competence

As stated earlier, over the years many different ideas and definitions of what constitutes culturally competent practice have developed, as indicated by the growth of the professional literature since the late 1970s. To date, focus has primarily been placed in two areas: (1) the need for practitioners to be aware or their own cultural beliefs, ideas, and identities leading to cultural sensitivity, and (2) learning factual and descriptive information about various ethnic and racial groups based mostly on group-level survey data and analyses. Fong (2001) suggests that culture is often considered "tangential" to individual functioning and not central to the client's functioning (p. 5).

To address this issue, Fong (2001) builds on Lum's (1999) culturally competent practice model that focuses on four areas: (1) cultural awareness, (2) knowledge acquisition, (3) skill development, and (4) inductive learning. Besides inductive learning, Lum's model focuses mainly on practitioners in perpetual self-awareness, gaining knowledge about cultures, and skill building. While these are important ideas for cultural competence, Fong (2001) calls for a shift in thinking and practice, "to provide a culturally competent service focused solely on the client rather than the social worker and what he or she brings to the awareness of ethnicity" (p. 5). Fong (2001) suggests an "extension" (p. 6) of Lum's model by turning the focus of each of the four elements away from the practitioner toward the client. For example, cultural awareness changes from a practitioner focus to "the social worker's understanding and the identification of the critical cultural values important to the client system and to themselves" (p. 6). This change allows Fong (2001) to remain consistent with the stated definition of culturally competent practice, insisting that practitioners,

> . . . operating from an empowerment, strengths, and ecological framework, provide services, conduct assessments, and implement interventions that are reflective of the clients' cultural values and norms, congruent with their natural help-seeking behaviors, and inclusive of existing indigenous solutions. (p. 1)

While we agree with the idea that "to be culturally competent is to know the cultural values of the client-system and to use them in planning and implementing services" (Fong, 2001, p. 6), we want to make this shift the main point of a culturally competent model of client engagement. That is, beyond what should or must occur, we believe that professional education and training must focus on the skills of culturally competent client engagement that are necessary to make this happen. This model places individual client cultural information at the center of practice. We agree with Fong (2001) that having culturally sensitive or culturally aware practitioners is not nearly enough. Practitioner self-awareness and knowledge of different cultures does not constitute cultural competence. We strive to find a method for reaching this worthy goal.

The central issue revolves around practitioners participating in inductive learning and the skills of grounded theory. In other words, regardless of practitioner beliefs, awarenesses, or sensitivities, their job is to learn about and understand their client's world, and to "ground" their theory of practice in the cultural context of their client. They develop a unique theory of human behavior in a multi-systemic context for every client. Culturally competent client engagement does not happen by assessing the extent to which client lives "fit" within existing theory and knowledge about reality, most of which is middle-class and Eurocentric at its core. Cultural competence (Johnson, 2004)

> . . . *begins* with learning about different cultures, races, personal circumstances, and structural mechanisms of oppression. It *occurs* when practitioners master the interpersonal skills needed to move beyond general descriptions of a specific culture or race to learn specific individual, family, group, or community interpretations of culture, ethnicity, and race. The culturally competent practitioner knows that within each culture are individually interpreted and practiced thoughts, beliefs, and behaviors that may or may not be consistent with group-level information. That is, there is tremendous diversity within groups, as well as between them. Individuals are unique unto themselves, not simply interchangeable members of a specific culture, ethnicity, or race who naturally abide by the group-level norms often taught on graduate and undergraduate courses on human diversity. (p. 105)

Culturally competent client engagement revolves around the practitioner's ability to create a relationship, through the professional use of self, based in true dialogue (Freire, 1993; Johnson, 2004). We define dialogue as "a joint endeavor, developed between people (in this case, practitioner and client) that move clients from their current state of hopelessness to a more hopeful, motivated position in their world" (Johnson, 2004, p. 97). Elsewhere (Johnson, 2004), we detailed a model of culturally competent engagement based on Freire's (1993) definitions of oppression, communication, dialogue, practitioner self-work, and the ability to exhibit worldview respect, hope, humility, trust, and empathy.

To investigate culture in a competent manner is to take a comprehensive look into people's worldviews—to discover what they believe about the world and their place in it. It goes beyond race and ethnicity (although these are important issues) into how culture determines thoughts, feelings, and behaviors in daily life. This includes what culture says about people's problems; culturally appropriate strengths and resources; the impact of gender on these issues; and what it means to seek professional help (Leigh, 1998).

The larger questions to be answered are how clients uniquely and individually interpret their culture; how their beliefs, attitudes, and behaviors are shaped by that interpretation; and how these cultural beliefs and practices affect daily life and determine lifestyle in the context of the larger community. Additionally, based on their cultural membership, beliefs, and practices, practitioners need to discover the potential and real barriers faced by clients in the world. Many clients, because they are part of non-majority cultures, are exposed to limitations and barriers that others do not face—issues such as racism, sexism, homophobia, and ethnocentrism.

What is the value of culturally competent client engagement? Helping clients discuss their attitudes, beliefs, and behaviors in the context of their culture—including their religious or spiritual belief systems—offers valuable information about their worldview, sense of social and spiritual connection, and/or practical involvement in their social world. Moreover, establishing connections between their unique interpretation of their culture and their daily life provides vital clues about people's belief systems, attitudes, expectations (social construction of reality), and explanation of behaviors that cannot be understood outside the context of their socially constructed interpretation of culture.

A Cautionary Note

It is easy to remember to ask about culture when clients are obviously different (i.e., different races, countries of origin, etc.). However, many practitioners forgo cultural investigation with clients they consider to have the same cultural background as the practitioner. For example, the search for differences between European Americans with Christian beliefs—if the social worker shares these characteristics—gets lost in mutual assumptions, based on the misguided belief that there are no important differences between them. The same is often true when clients and practitioners come from the same racial, cultural, or lifestyle backgrounds (i.e., African American practitioner and client, gay practitioner and gay client, etc.). Culturally competent practice means that practitioners are always interested in people's individual interpretation of their culture and their subjective definitions of reality, whether potential differences are readily apparent or not. Practitioners must be diligent to explore culture with clients who appear to be from the same background as the practitioner, just as they would with people who are obviously from different cultural, racial, ethnic, or religious backgrounds.

Multiple Theories and Methods

No single theory, model, or method is best suited to meet the needs of all clients (Miley, O'Melia, & DuBois, 2004). Consistent with this statement, one of the hallmarks of AMS is the expectation that practitioners must determine which theory, model, or method will best suit a particular client. Choosing from a range of approaches and interventions, AMS practitioners develop the skills and abilities to: (1) determine which treatment approach (theory and/or method) would best suit their needs and achieve the desired outcome, based on the client's life, history, culture, and style, (2) decide which modality or modalities (individual, family, group treatment, etc.) will best meet the need of their clients, and (3) conduct treatment according to their informed clinical decisions.

Over the last 20 years or so, graduate social work education has trended toward practice specialization through concentration-based curricula. Many graduate schools of social work build on the generalist foundation by insisting that students focus on learning specific practice models or theories (disease, cognitive-behavioral, psychoanalysis, etc.) and/or specific practice methods (individual, family, group, etc.)—often at the exclusion of other methods or models. For example, students often enter the field intent on doing therapy with individuals, say, from a cognitive-behavioral approach only.

This trend encourages practitioners to believe that one approach or theory best represents the "Truth." Truth, in this sense, is the belief that one theory or approach works best for most people, most of the time. It helps create a practice scenario that leads practitioners to use their chosen approach with every client they treat. Therefore, practice becomes a process of the practitioner forcing clients to adjust to the practitioner's beliefs and expectations about the nature of problems, the course of treatment, and definition of positive versus negative outcomes. From this perspective, what is best for clients is determined by what the practitioner believes is best, not what clients believe is in their best interest.

Some practitioners take their belief in the Truth of a particular theory or method to extremes. They believe that one model or theory works best for all people, all the time. We found this to be common in the family therapy field, whereby some true believers insist that everyone needs family therapy—so that is all they offer. What's worse is that many of these same practitioners know and use only one particular family therapy theory and model. The "true believer" approach can cause problems, especially for clients. For example, when clients do not respond to treatment, instead of looking to other approaches, true believers simply prescribe more of the method that did not work in the first place. If a more intensive application of the method does not work, then the client's "lack of readiness" for treatment, resistance, or denial becomes the culprit. These practitioners usually give little thought to their practice approach or personal style and its impact on client "readiness" for treatment. They fail to examine the role their personal style, beliefs, attitudes, and practices have in creating the context that led to clients not succeeding in treatment.

Each practice theory and model has a relatively unique way of defining client problems, practitioner method and approach, interventions, and what constitutes successful outcome. For practitioners to believe that one theory or model is true, even if only for most people, they must believe in the universality of problems, methods, approaches, interventions, and successful outcome criteria. This contradicts the definition of theory. While being far from a concrete representation of the truth, a theory is a set of myths, expectations, guesses, and conjectures about what might be true (Best & Kellner, 1991). A theory is hypothetical; a set of ideas and explanations that need proving. No single theory can explain everything. According to Popper (1994), a theory ". . . always remains guesswork, and there is no theory that is not beset with problems" (p. 157). As such, treatment specialization can—although not always—encourage people to believe they have found the Truth where little truth exists.

Practitioners using an AMS perspective come to believe that some element of every established practice model, method, or theory may be helpful. Accordingly, every model, method, or theory can be adapted and used in a multi-systemic practice framework. As an AMS practitioner, one neither accepts any single model fully, nor disregards a model entirely if there is potential for helping a client succeed in a way that is compatible with professional social work values and ethics. These practitioners hone their critical thinking skills (Gambrill, 1997, 1990) and apply them in practice, particularly as it pertains to treatment theories, models, and methods. In the context of evidence-based practice (Cournoyer, 2004; Gibbs, 2003), sharpened critical thinking skills allow practitioners to closely read and evaluate practice theories, research, or case reports. These in turn help practitioners to recognize the strengths, weakness, and contradictions in theories, models, and/or policy related to social work practice.

Informed Eclecticism

The goal of AMS related to treatment methods is for practitioners to develop an approach we call *informed eclecticism.* Informed eclecticism allows the use of multiple methods, interventions, and approaches in the context of practice that is held together by a perspective or approach that provides consistency and that makes practice choices in a way that makes sense in a particular client's life. This approach is based, whenever possible, on the latest evidence about its efficacy with particular problems and particular clients. While it is often best to rely on empirical evidence, this data is in its infancy. AMS does not preclude the use of informed practice wisdom and personal creativity in developing intervention plans and approaches. It is up to practitioners to ensure that any treatment that is based in practice wisdom or that is creatively generated be discussed with colleagues, supervisors, or consultants. This will ensure theoretical consistency and will help the practitioner adhere to the code of professional ethics.

Informed eclecticism is different from the routine definition of eclecticism—the use of whatever theory, model, or method works best for their clients. While this is the goal of AMS practice specifically and social work practice in general (Timberlake, Farber, & Sabatino, 2002), it is an elusive goal indeed. Informed eclecticism often gets lost in a practitioner's quest to find something that "works." According to Gambrill (1997), eclecticism is "the view that we should adopt whatever theories or methodologies is useful in inquiry, no matter what their source and without worry about their consistency" (p. 93). The most important word in Gambrill's statement is "consistency." While there are practitioners who have managed to develop a consistent, organized, and holistic version of informed eclecticism, this is not the norm.

Too often, uninformed eclecticism resembles the following. Many practitioners specialize in modality (individual therapy) and use a variety of modality-specific ideas and practices in their work with clients. They change ideas and tactics when the approach they normally use does not "work." This often leaves the practitioner searching (mostly in vain) for the magic intervention—what "works." Moreover, while uninformed eclectic practitioners use interventions from various "schools," they remain primarily wedded to one modality. Hence, they end up confusing themselves and their clients as they search for the "right" approach, rarely looking beyond their chosen modality, and outside of their self-imposed, theoretical cage.

For example, an uninformed eclectic practitioner specializing in individual therapy may try a cognitive approach, a client-centered approach, a Freudian approach, or a behavioral approach. A family therapy specialist may use a structural, strategic, or solution-focused approach. However, in the end, little changes. These practitioners still believe that their clients need individual or family treatment. They rarely consider potentially useful ideas and tactics taken from different modalities that could be used instead of, or in combination with, an individual or family approach, mostly because they base treatment decisions on their chosen modality.

While informed eclecticism is the goal, most find it difficult to find consistency when trying to work from a variety of models at the same time. The informed eclectic practitioners, through experience and empirical evidence, have a unifying approach that serves as the basis for using different models or methods. What is important, according to clinical outcome research, is the consistency of approach in helping facilitate successful client outcome (Gaston, 1990; Miller & Rollnick, 2002; Harper & Lantz, 1996). Trying to be eclectic makes consistency (and treatment success), quite difficult.

What uninformed eclecticism lacks is the framework needed to gain a holistic and comprehensive understanding of the client in the context of his or her life, history, and multiple environments. This understanding leads naturally to culturally consistent treatment and intervention decisions. AMS, as it is described here, provides such a framework. It is holistic, integrative, ecological, and based in the latest empirical evidence. It is an inclusive framework that bases treatment decisions on a multi-systemic assessment of specific client history and culture. It is designed, whenever possible, to capitalize on client strengths, to be consistent with culturally specific help-seeking behavior, and to utilize existing or formulated community-based and/or natural support systems in the client's environment.

Defining Multi-Systemic Client Information

In this section we specifically discuss the different dimensions that comprise AMS practice. This is a general look at what constitutes multi-systemic client life information. There are six levels of information that, when integrated into a life history of clients, demonstrates how multiple theories, models, and approaches can be applied to better understand, assess, and treat clients or client-systems. Generally, the six dimensions (biological, psychological, family, religious/spiritual/existential, social/environmental, and macro) encompass a range of information needed to complete a comprehensive, multi-systemic assessment, treatment, and intervention plan with client-systems of all sizes and configurations.

1. Biological Dimension

AMS practitioners need to understand what some have called the "mind-body connection," or the links between social/emotional, behavioral, and potential biological or genetic issues that may be, at least in part, driving the problems presented by clients in practice. As scientific evidence mounts regarding the biological and genetic sources of personal troubles (i.e., some mental illness), it grows imperative for well-trained AMS practitioners to apply this knowledge in everyday work with clients (Ginsberg, Nackerud, & Larrison, 2004). The responsibility for understanding biology and physical health goes well beyond those working in direct healthcare practice settings (i.e., hospital, HIV, or hospice practice settings). Issues pertaining to physical health confront practitioners in all practice settings.

For example, practitioners working in mental health settings are confronted daily with issues pertaining to human biology. These issues include the sources and determinants of mental illness, differential uses of psychotropic medication, and often, the role played in client behavior by proper nutrition, appropriate health care, and even physical rest. In foster care and/or family preservation, practitioners also confront the effects of parental abuses (i.e., fetal alcohol syndrome [FAS]), medication management, and child/adolescent physical and biological development issues.

Beyond learning about the potential biological or physical determinants of various client troubles, having a keen understanding of the potential physical and health risks associated with various behaviors and/or lifestyles places practitioners in the position of intervening to save lives. For example, practitioners working with substance abusing or chemically dependent clients must understand drug pharmacology—especially drug-mixing—to predict potentially life-threatening physical withdrawal effects and/or to prevent intentional or unintentional harm caused by drug overdose (Johnson, 2004).

AMS requires that practitioners keep current with the latest information about human biology, development, genetics, and potential associated health risks facing clients and client-systems in practice. With that knowledge, practitioners can include this information during client assessment, treatment planning, and intervention strategies. It also requires practitioners to know the limits of professional responsibility. That is, social workers are not physicians and should never offer medical advice or guidance that is not supported by properly trained physicians. Therefore, AMS practitioners utilize the appropriate medical professionals as part of assessment, planning, and intervention processes with all clients.

2. Psychological/Emotional Dimension

AMS practitioners need a working knowledge of the ways that psychological and emotional functioning are intertwined with clients' problems and strengths, how issues from this dimension contribute to the way their client or client-system interacts with self and others in their environment, and how their environments influence their psychological and emotional functioning. There are several important skill sets that practitioners must develop to consider issues in this dimension. First, being able to recognize potential problems through a mental screening examination is a skill necessary to all practitioners. Also, having a keen understanding of the *Diagnostic and Statistical Manual of Mental Disorders* (DSM) (American Psychological Association, 2000), including the multi-axial diagnostic process, and recognition of the limits of this tool in the overall multi-systemic assessment process is instrumental. Especially critical is the ability to recognize co-occurring disorders (Johnson, 2004). It is also valuable to learn the Person-in-Environment (PIE) assessment system (Karls & Wandrei, 1994a, 1994b), a diagnostic model developed specifically for social workers to incorporate environmental influences.

In addition to understanding how psychology and emotion affects client mood and behavior, AMS practitioners also know how to employ different theories and models used for treating psychological and emotional functioning problems in the context of a client's multi-systemic assessment and treatment plan. This includes methods of treating individuals, families, and groups. Depending on the client's multi-systemic assessment, each of these modalities or some combination of modalities is appropriate for people with problems in this dimension.

3. Family Dimension

The family is the primary source of socialization, modeling, and nurturing of children. Hence, the family system has a significant impact on people's behavior, and people's behavior has significant impact on the health and well-being of their family system (Johnson, 2004). By integrating a family systems perspective into AMS, practitioners will often be able to make sense of behavior attitudes, beliefs, and values that would otherwise be difficult to understand or explain.

For our purposes, a family is defined as a group of people—regardless of their actual blood or legal relationship—whom clients consider to be members of their family (Johnson, 2004). This definition is designed to privilege clients' perceptions and subjective construction of reality and avoid disagreements over who is or is not in someone's family. So, if a client refers to a neighbor as "Uncle Joe," then that perception represents their reality. What good would it do to argue otherwise? Just as in client engagement discussed earlier, AMS practitioners seek to understand and embrace their client's unique definition of family, rather than imposing a rigid standard that may not fit their perceived reality. This is especially important when dealing with gay and lesbian clients. The law may not recognize gay or lesbian marriage, but AMS practitioners must, if that is the nature of the client's relationship and consistent with their belief system.

It is important to have a working knowledge of different theories and approaches to assessing and treating families and couples. Practitioners should possess the ability to construct three-generation genograms to help conceptualize family systems and characterize the relationships that exist within the family system and between the family and its environment. Family treatment requires unique skills, specialized post-graduate training, and regular supervision before practitioners can master the methods and call themselves "family therapists." However, the journey toward mastery is well worth it. Family treatment can be among the most effective and meaningful treatment modalities. It is often used in conjunction with other modalities (individual and/or group treatment), or can be used as the primary treatment method.

4. Religious/Spiritual/Existential Dimension

Practitioners, students, and social work educators are often wary of exploring issues related to religion and spirituality in practice or the classroom. While there are exceptions, this important dimension often goes unexamined. Exploring people's religious beliefs and/or the tenets of their faith, as they pertain to people's subjective definition of self in relation to the world is an important part of AMS practice. This is important even if people do not appear to have faith or spiritual beliefs.

How clients view themselves in relation to others and their world provides an interesting window into the inner workings of their individual interpretation of culture. The extent that clients have internalized messages (positive, negative, and/or neutral) about their behavior from their faith community or personal spiritual belief systems can lead to an understanding of why people approach their lives and others in the ways they do. Moreover, much can be learned, based on these beliefs, about people's belief in the potential for change, how change occurs, and whom is best suited to help in that change process (if anyone at all), especially as it relates to the many moral and religious messages conveyed about people with problems.

Examination of this dimension goes beyond discovering which church or synagogue clients attend. It is designed to learn how and by what means clients define themselves and their lives in their worlds. Practitioners can discover what tenets clients use to justify their lives, and how these tenets either support their current lives or can be used to help lead them toward change. There is much to be learned about client culture, how people interpret their culture in daily life, and how they view their life in their personal context from an examination of their religious or spiritual beliefs.

Moreover, religious and spiritual belief systems can also be a source of strength and support when considered in treatment plans. For example, while many clients may benefit from attendance at a community support group (i.e., Alcoholics Anonymous, Overeaters Anonymous, etc.) or from professional treatment, some will benefit even more from participation in groups and events through local houses of worship. In our experience, many clients unable to succeed in professional treatment or support groups found success through a connection or reconnection with organizations that share their faith, whatever that faith may be.

5. Social/Environmental Dimension

Beyond the individual and family, AMS practitioners look to the client's community, including the physical environment, for important clues to help with engagement, assessment, and intervention planning. People live in communities comprised of three different types: (1) location (neighborhoods, cities, and rural or urban villages), (2) identification (religion, culture, race, etc.), and (3) affiliation (group memberships, subcultures, professional, political/ideological groups, etc.). There are five subdimensions that comprise the social/environmental dimension and incorporate the three types of communities listed above (Johnson, 2004).

1. Local community.   This includes learning about physical environment, living conditions, a person's fit within *her* community, neighborhoods, where and how people live on a daily basis, and how they believe they are treated and/or accepted by community members and the community's power structure (i.e., the police, etc.).

2. Cultural context.   This includes learning about clients' larger culture, their individual interpretation of culture, and how it drives or influences their daily life. Also included here is an exploration of histories of oppression and discrimination (individual, family, and community) and a client's subcultural group membership (i.e., drug culture, gang culture, etc.).

3. Social class.   Often overlooked by practitioners, "information about people's social class is directly related to information about their families, the goodness-of-fit between the person and environment, and the strengths, resources, and/or barriers in their communities" (Johnson, 2004, p. 226). Some believe that no other demographic factor explains so extensively the differences between people and/or groups (Lipsitz, 1997; Davis & Proctor, 1989). Social class represents a combination of income, education, occupation, prestige, and community. It encompasses how these factors affect people's relative wealth and access to power and opportunity (Johnson, 2004).

4. Social/relational. Human beings are social creatures who define themselves in relation to others (Johnson, 2004). Therefore, it is necessary to know something about people's ability to relate to others in their social environment. This investigation includes loved ones, friends, peers, supervisors, teachers, and others that they relate to in their daily life.

5. Legal history and involvement. Obviously, this subdimension includes information about involvement with the legal system by the client, family members, and friends and peers. More than recording a simple demographic history, seek to discover their feelings, attitudes, and beliefs about themselves, their place in the world, and how their brushes with the law fit into or influence their worldview.

6. Community resources. Investigate the nature and availability of organizational support, including the role of social service organizations, politics, and your presence as a social worker in a client's life. For example, can clients find a program to serve their needs, or what does seeing a social worker mean within their community or culture? What are the conditions of the schools and the influence of churches, neighborhood associations, and block clubs? More importantly, what is the prevailing culture of the local environment? Are neighbors supportive or afraid of each other, and can a client expect to reside in the present situation and receive the support needed to change?

Be sure to include the professional helping system in this subdimension. Practitioners, their agencies, and the policies that assist or impede the professional helping process join with client-systems as part of the overall system in treatment. In other words, we must consider ourselves as part of the system—we do not stand outside in objective observation. This includes practitioner qualities and styles, agency policies, broader policies related to specific populations, and reimbursement policies, including managed care. All of these factors routinely influence the extent to which clients receive help, how clients are perceived in the helping system and, in the case of reimbursement policies, the method of treatment clients are eligible to receive regardless of how their multi-systemic assessment turns out.

Familiarity with various theories and models of community provide the keys to understanding the role of the social, physical, political, and economic environment in an individual's life. Community models look at the broader environment and its impact on people. Clients or client-systems with issues located in this dimension often respond well to group and family treatment methods. Occasionally, practitioners will be required to intervene at the local neighborhood or community level through organizing efforts and/or personal or political advocacy. For example:

> I (Johnson) was treating a client in individual and occasional family treatment when it was discovered that the daughter had been molested by a neighbor. The parents had not reported the molestation. I soon learned that this neighbor was rumored to have molested several young girls in the neighborhood and that nobody was willing to report the molestations. I urged my client to organize a neighborhood meeting of all

involved parents at her home. I served as the group facilitator for an intense meeting that ultimately built the community support needed to involve law enforcement. Within days, all of the parents in this group met with law enforcement. The perpetrator was arrested, convicted, and sentenced to life imprisonment.

6. Macro Dimension

AMS practitioners do not stop looking for relevant client information at the local level. They also look for clues in the way that macro issues influence clients, their problems, and potential for change. Knowledge of various laws (local, state, and national) are critical, as well as an understanding of how various social policies are interpreted and enforced in a particular client's life. For example, AMS requires an understanding of how child welfare policies affect the life of a chemically dependent mother, how healthcare policy affects a family's decisions about seeking medical treatment for their children, or how local standards of hygiene or cleanliness affect a family's status and acceptance in their community.

Issues to consider at this level also include public sentiment, stereotypes, and mechanisms of oppression that play a significant role in the lives of people who are not Caucasian, male, middle-class (or more affluent) citizens. Racism, classism, homophobia, and sexism, to name a few, are real threats to people who are attempting to live a "normal" life. An AMS practitioner must understand this reality and learn from clients what their individual perceptions are of these mechanisms and how they affect their problems and potential for change. The macro dimension involves issues such as housing, employment, and public support, along with the dynamics of the criminal justice system. For example, if clients have been arrested for domestic violence, what is the chance they will get fair and just legal representation? If they have been convicted and served jail or prison sentences, what are the chances they will have a reasonable chance of finding sufficient employment upon release?

These issues can be addressed in individual, family, or group treatments. Often, group treatment is an effective way to address issues clients struggle with at the macro level. Group treatment provides clients a way to address these issues in the context of mutual social support and a sense of belonging by helping clients realize that they are not alone in their struggles (Yalom, 1995). AMS practitioners also recognize the need for political advocacy and community organizing methods for clients who consistently struggle with issues at the macro level.

Summary

The hallmark of AMS is its reliance on and integration of multi-systemic client information into one comprehensive assessment, treatment, and intervention plan. It incorporates knowledge, skills, and values from multiple sources, and relies on various sources of knowledge to paint a holistic picture of people's lives, struggles, strengths, resources, and potentials for change. Practitioners need a current working knowledge of human behavior, social systems theories, the latest social research and practice evaluation results, and the impact of public laws and policies. They also need the skills and abilities to plan and implement treatment approaches as needed, in a manner consistent with our definition of informed eclecticism.

Many students new to AMS start out confused because the requirements seem so diverse and complicated. However, as you will see in the case presentations to follow, an organized and efficient practitioner who has learned to think and act multi-systemically can gather large amounts of critically important information about a client in a relatively short period. For this to happen, you must have a deep understanding of various theories, models, and practice approaches that address the various systemic levels. You should be willing to accept that no single model is completely right or wrong. It is always easier to latch on to one model and "go with it." However, the goal of practice is not to be correct or to promote your own ease and comfort, but to develop an assessment and treatment plan that is right for each client, whether or not you would ever use it in your own life. Social work practice is not about the social worker, but the client. It is important never to lose sight of this fact.

Bibliography

American Psychiatric Association (2000). *Diagnostic and statistical manual of mental disorders* (4th ed., TR). Washington, DC: Author.

Appleby, G. A. (2001). Dynamics of oppression and discrimination. In G. A. Appleby, E. Colon, & J. Hamilton (eds.), *Diversity, oppression, and social functioning: Person-in-environment assessment and intervention*. Boston: Allyn and Bacon.

Best, S., & Kellner, D. (1991). *Postmodern theory: Critical interrogations*. New York: Guilford Press.

Cournoyer, B. R. (2004). *The evidence-based social work skills book*. Boston: Allyn and Bacon.

Cox, E. O., & Parsons, R. J. (1994). *Empowerment-oriented social work practice with the elderly*. Pacific Grove, CA: Brooks/Cole.

Davis, L. E., & Proctor, E. K. (1989). *Race, gender, and class: Guidelines for practice with individuals, families, and groups*. Englewood Cliffs, NJ: Prentice-Hall.

Derezotes, D. S. (2000). *Advanced generalist social work practice*. Thousand Oaks, CA: Sage.

Fong, R. (2001). Culturally competent social work practice: Past and present. In R. Fong & S. Furuto (eds.), *Culturally competent practice: Skills, interventions, and evaluations*. Boston: Allyn and Bacon.

Freire, P. (1993). *Pedagogy of the oppressed*. New York: Continuum.

Gambrill, E. (1997). *Social work practice: A critical thinker's guide*. New York: Oxford University Press.

Gambrill, E. (1990). *Critical thinking in clinical practice*. San Francisco: Jossey-Bass.

Gaston, L. (1990). The concept of the alliance and its role in psychotherapy: Theoretical and empirical considerations. *Psychotherapy, 27,* 143–153.

Geertz, C. (1973). *The interpretation of cultures*. New York: Basic Books.

Germain, C. B., & Gitterman, A. (1996). *The life model of social work practice* (2nd ed.). New York: Columbia University Press.

Germain, C. B., & Gitterman, A. (1980). *The ecological model of social work practice*. New York: Columbia University Press.

Gibbs, L. E. (2003). *Evidence-based practice for the helping professions: A practical guide with integrated multimedia.* Pacific Grove, CA: Brooks/Cole.

Ginsberg, L., Nackerud, L., & Larrison, C. R. (2004). *Human biology for social workers: Development, ecology, genetics, and health.* Boston: Allyn and Bacon.

GlenMaye, L. (1998). Empowerment of women. In L. M. Gutierrez, R. J. Parsons, & E. O. Cox (eds.), *Empowerment in social work practice: A sourcebook.* Pacific Grove, CA: Brooks/Cole.

Gordon, J. U. (1993). A culturally specific approach to ethnic minority young adults. In E. M. Freeman (ed.), *Substance abuse treatment: A family systems perspective.* Newbury Park, CA: Sage.

Greif, G. L. (1986). The ecosystems perspective "meets the press." *Social Work, 31,* 225–226.

Harper, K. V., & Lantz, J. (1996). *Cross-cultural practice: Social work practice with diverse populations.* Chicago: Lyceum Books.

Johnson, J. L. (2004). *Fundamentals of substance abuse practice.* Pacific Grove, CA: Brooks/Cole.

Johnson, J. L. (2000). *Crossing borders—Confronting history: Intercultural adjustment in a post-Cold War world.* Lanham, MD: University Press of America.

Karls, J., & Wandrei, K. (1994a). *Person-in-environment system: The PIE classification system for functioning problems.* Washington, DC: NASW.

Karls, J., & Wandrei, K. (1994b). *PIE manual: Person-in-environment system: The PIE classification system for social functioning.* Washington, DC: NASW.

Kozol, J. (1991). *Savage inequalities: Children in America's schools.* New York: Crown Publishers.

Leigh, J. W. (1998). *Communicating for cultural competence.* Boston: Allyn and Bacon.

Lipsitz, G. (1997). Class and class consciousness: Teaching about social class in public universities. In A. Kumar (ed.), *Class issues.* New York: New York University Press.

Longres, J. F. (2000). *Human behavior in the social environment* (3rd ed.). Itasca, IL: F. E. Peacock.

Lum, D. (1999). *Culturally competent practice.* Pacific Grove, CA: Brooks/Cole.

McLaren, P. (1995). *Critical pedagogy and predatory culture: Oppositional politics in a postmodern era.* London: Routledge.

Miley, K. K., O'Melia, M., & DuBois, B. (2004). *Generalist social work practice: An empowerment approach.* Boston: Allyn and Bacon.

Miller, W. R., & Rollnick, S. (2002). *Motivational interviewing: Preparing people to change addictive behavior* (2nd ed.). New York: Guilford Press.

Mills, C. W. (1959). *The sociological imagination.* New York: Oxford University Press.

Parsons, R. J., Gutierrez, L. M., & Cox, E. O. (1998). A model for empowerment practice. In L. M. Gutierrez, R. J. Parsons, & E. O. Cox (eds.), *Empowerment in social work practice: A sourcebook.* Pacific Grove, CA: Brooks/Cole.

Pinderhughes, E. (1989). *Understanding race, ethnicity, and power.* New York: Free Press.

Popper, K. R. (1994). *The myth of the framework: In defense of science and rationality.* Edited by M. A. Notturno. New York: Routledge.

Saleebey, D. (2002). *The strengths perspective in social work practice* (3rd ed.). Boston: Allyn and Bacon.

Smelser, N. J. (1992). Culture: Coherent or incoherent. In R. Munch & N. J. Smelser (eds.), *Theory of culture.* Berkeley, CA: University of California Press.

Timberlake, E. M., Farber, M. Z., & Sabatino, C. A. (2002). *The general method of social work practice: McMahon's generalist perspective* (4th ed.). Boston: Allyn and Bacon.

van Wormer, K., & Davis, D. R. (2003). *Addiction treatment: A strengths perspective.* Pacific Grove, CA: Brooks/Cole.

Yalom, I. (1995). *The theory and practice of group psychotherapy* (4th ed.). New York: Basic Books.

2

Crisis and Kinship in Foster Care

Kathy A. Miller

Introduction

When you look back on a case, you see the entire problem with its unexpected twists and turns, and you know the answer to all the questions. However, whatever your education and training, social work doesn't come with all the answers at the beginning of a case. What we hope to bring to every case is the ability to assess, engage, problem solve, provide hope, and assist those in need.

One of the tenets of child welfare is the placement of children in the least restrictive placement possible. This means that when a child can't live with his or her parents, the setting closest to that setting should be found. When the parents are unable or unwilling to provide that care, a relative placement is the next least restrictive. However, there are times when a relative placement is not the best placement.

The Raney family is one of those cases. The Raney family came to the attention of the County's Child Welfare Division following a drug raid to the mother's home. The police called Children's Protective Services and they picked up three children in the home at the time. The Raney children—Lucy, six years old; Robert, three years old; and Joey, 20 months old—were sleeping on a mattress on the floor when the police arrested their mother, Blanche, for maintaining a drug house. The police also arrested and charged two men in the home with drug crimes.

At the time of her arrest, Blanche told the Children's Protective Services worker that she had no family to care for the children. The children were therefore placed in licensed foster care by means of an emergency placement order from the juvenile court. At a preliminary hearing the next day, the children continued their stay in foster care and were officially put in the temporary custody of the court pending the neglect trial.

After the court hearing, the case transferred from the investigation branch of the agency (Children's Protective Services) to the foster care division. As the foster care worker assigned to the family, it became my primary objective to provide necessary services to the family to help them overcome any barriers to providing proper care for the children. It appeared from the brief information available at the time of the case transfer that this would be a rather "typical" case involving substance abuse and child neglect issues.

One of the most difficult aspects in child welfare work is establishing rapport with the client. There is an institutional type barrier relating to building a relationship and engaging with the client. The same agency that petitioned the court for removal of the children then, by the change of a caseworker and agency division, has the obligation of forming a positive therapeutic relationship with the client and establishing trust with the goal of assisting the family in reunification efforts. This is an underlying supposition in any new case and was anticipated in this case, as well. In court-ordered cases, a helping relationship would take more time to build than in other areas of social work practice due to this built-in dilemma.

Law and policy, however, dictate a relatively short timeframe for the resolution of a foster care case. The *Child Protective Proceedings Benchbook* describes the law mandating the permanency guidelines as follows: "The child's supervising agency is required to strive to achieve a permanent placement for the child, including either a safe return to the child's home or implementation of an alternate permanency plan, within 12 months after the child is removed from his or her home" (Miller, 1999, p. 17). In almost all cases, the hopeful outcome is reunification with the parent. An alternative plan, such as termination of parental rights and eventual adoption, is an option when reunification fails.

The knowledge of these timeframes dictated that assessment and intervention would have to be undertaken quickly and sometimes simultaneously. While gathering assessment information, some forms of treatment intervention were already taking place. While set forth as separate in this case, the reader should not assume that in the actual casework the lines between the stages of progression were so cleanly delineated.

Assessment

Home and Community

Assessment in foster care cases is an ongoing process, developing at many levels. As situations in the case and family change, assessments are continually updated. An integral part of the assessment to complete initially is a study of the home and community from which the children were removed. The dynamics of how the family relates within these confines and how the various systems interplay are dependent upon an understanding of this basic aspect.

My work in the community provided me with extensive knowledge of the area. The Raney family lived in a rural community. The population of this community was primarily of Mexican descent, many of whom settled into the area from migrant farm work. Much of the housing was considered substandard by comparison with other areas and included former "farm camp" housing and older modular type dwellings. The families were primarily low-income and many were dependent on financial assistance from the payments assistance units of the same social services agency that was involved in the child protective proceedings. The area was reputed for its proliferation of drug activity, especially marijuana and crack cocaine. Teenage gang activity was also common to the area.

The situation that brought the Raneys to the attention of social services was similar to other drug cases. The agency often became involved in cases in which poor women under similar situations became dependent on men who manufactured or sold drugs. This relationship allowed them to sustain a drug habit they could not afford. The men would often take residence and sell drugs out of the woman's subsidized housing. Aside from the evident problems relating to parenting while abusing substances, the traffic and personnel frequenting the home presented a real danger to children in the home. As in Blanche's case, this often left the woman facing criminal charges for maintaining a drug house, losing her housing, and having her children placed in foster care for neglect or endangerment.

Questions

The author described a trend where women living in low-income housing get involved in relationships with men who sell drugs out of their homes.

1. From your review of the professional literature, what factors contribute to these women allowing the sale of drugs out of their home?

2. From the literature, explain why these men are using women in low-income housing to sell their drugs?

3. If the women are involved in a relationship with these men, and know they are selling the drugs, are the women coconspirators or victims of the drug selling? Please explain your reasoning.

The Raney family, although surrounded by a neighborhood or community of other families, was isolated from services. Blanche had no driver's license and relied on others for transportation. There was a small "mom & pop" style grocery/liquor store in walking distance, however, that store was reputed for inflating prices. Health care, shopping, and other human service agencies were located within ten to fifteen miles of the neighborhood. The lack of public transportation in the rural area limited access to most services.

In addition to limitations caused by lack of formal education and training, this same isolation limited employment opportunities for residents of the community. Many of the families maintained at least seasonal work at local farms; however, even minimum wage food service positions were located outside of walking distance.

Those on the outside viewed the community as "secretive." Much of this assumption came from a language gap or barrier. The residents of this particular community spoke Spanish fluently, many as their first language. In most homes, Spanish was the primary language spoken. Conversations often included a mix of both Spanish and English. Those who spoke no Spanish, including the social services workers, at times thought the speakers were intentionally hiding something.

The community also provided a great source of support for its residents. Families provided day care for each other as needed. Each knew details about the neighbors and was known to open their doors for a neighbor or family should they need assistance. Churches appeared to be the cornerstone of the community. The largest church in the area was a Catholic church whose priest performed the Sunday morning mass in Spanish. The church housed a day care center and some teen programs.

Historically, the community viewed government intervention with skepticism. Many of the residents felt that the government had neither addressed their needs nor tried to develop their community. There was also concern that the legal system treated them unfairly and focused police efforts in their community, thereby leading to a high rate of arrests within the population.

Living Environment

Blanche Raney rented a home in this community. The home itself had one bedroom, a living room, kitchen, and bathroom. At the time of the initial investigation, it was found that the water was not working and bare wiring was noted throughout the home. Blanche was heating the home with her oven, as there was no other working heat source. The children slept on the single mattress on the floor near the kitchen to take advantage of the heat source.

The kitchen sink was full of dirty dishes and garbage laid strewn throughout the home. The water had been shut off due to nonpayment of the utility bill. The bathroom plumbing was, therefore, nonfunctional. Soiled diapers were heaped into the toilet and onto the bathroom floor. The condition of the children's clothing and toys made it impossible to take anything of theirs to the foster home.

Also living in the home was the mother's boyfriend, Larry. Larry was not the father of any of the children and was unemployed. Larry was arrested in a raid along with his brother. They were both charged for the sale of crack cocaine and also faced weapons charges.

It appeared that the situation within the mother's home was not appropriate for the children due to health and safety issues regardless of the drug raid. Health and safety issues surrounding the condition of the home were evident. Therefore, in addition to the original complaint, which necessitated the children's removal, the mother was also charged with child neglect.

Kinship Assessment

I received a call from Blanche's brother and sister-in-law the next day. They requested that the children be placed with them. They lived in the same community as Blanche and had three children of their own. Blanche's brother, Nestor, claimed that neighbors who reported that Blanche was arrested called him and told him that the children were placed in foster care. When informed that his sister had not provided any relatives' names for the children's placement, he said, "we had been estranged for the past few months due to her involvement with Larry."

The family was denied placement after an initial home study. Although the home was clean and did not appear to contain the safety hazards of Blanche's home, it had only two bedrooms. The parents slept in one bedroom with the baby, and two older children slept in the other. The older Raney children would have shared a room with their two cousins and the baby would stay in a crib in the living room. The family also often allowed other relatives to stay with them as necessary. It simply appeared that there was no physical space for the placement of the children.

Financial issues also appeared to be present in the family. Nestor was not employed, but received social security disability income. He stated that this was due to a back injury sustained in an auto accident five years prior. His wife spoke very little English and did not work outside of the home. From a quick study of the family's finances, it was clear that their monthly income was insufficient to meet all of their bills.

Nestor stated that he seldom paid the rent in full, as his landlord allowed him to do odd jobs on many of the rental properties in the community in exchange for full payment of rent. Therefore, he was able to meet the needs of his family with the social security income. He believed that he would be able to manage his sister's three children on the same budget.

The family also had a history of child abuse from two years prior. Nestor was adamant that he had not abused his son and that the "state" had no right to tell him how to discipline his children. The prior Children's Protective Services case involved spanking the oldest child with a belt and leaving marks. It appeared from case records that Nestor grudgingly completed a parenting class and the case was closed. All three of the children appeared to be well cared for with no apparent signs of abuse or neglect at the time of the home study.

When it is necessary to remove children from the parental home, it is most often preferable to place the children with relatives if possible. However, due to the Children's Protective Services history in this family, as well as the lack of space and financial limitations, it was decided that the children's best interests would be served by having them remain in licensed foster care placement.

Questions

1. The three Raney children could not be placed with the uncle because of his lack of space and financial resources. If the three children were his biological children, the lack of space and financial resources would not have been a problem. Why do you think this distinction exists?

2. In your state, are there laws that prevent relatives from having children placed in their home if they have a criminal record? What types of crimes would prevent relative placements? What are the exceptions to those laws?

Parent Assessment

There was no previous information available regarding Blanche and her family from protective services files. They had never been involved with the system in the past. From the referral information it was assumed, and Nestor verified, that Blanche was abusing drugs. He stated that she used marijuana and crack cocaine since becoming involved with Larry a year prior. It was this habit that caused her to mismanage her finances to the point of allowing Larry to move in and sell drugs out of her home. Nestor was protective of his sister, stating that the children's father had abandoned them and was living in Texas or Mexico. He stated that Blanche has always needed someone to take care of her.

Due to her incarceration, my first meeting with Blanche took place at the jail. She looked disheveled and distracted as we sat in the visiting room. Blanche was very quiet. Although she would answer questions posed to her, she would not elaborate on answers or offer information without being asked. It also appeared that Blanche was nervous, as she averted her eyes and would not maintain eye contact during the initial meeting. I assumed that given her current situation, she was likely embarrassed or nervous. I was also concerned that Blanche's seemingly avoidant nonverbal cues might be indicating that she was being less than truthful or forthcoming during the interview. However, the adversarial nature of her relationship with the agency had to be understood. Although I described the foster care position and goal as different from Children's Protective Services, clients viewed it as the same entity. In reality, they are the same place. We share client information while talking about cases, frustrations, and problem-solving difficult cases.

Blanche admitted that her boyfriend had a drug problem and that although he "stayed" at her house, they did not live together. Blanche stated that she had used drugs in the past but had quit. She also denied neglecting or abusing her children.

When asked what impact she perceived the drug raid had on her children, she stated, "They were asleep. They were not hurt by it." When asked about the condition of the home, Blanche stated that she and the children bathed and toileted at the neighbor's home. She denied that the housekeeping was substandard, it just happened to be dirty on the day of the removal. Since that was my first meeting with Blanche, I was sure she did not trust me. In addition to that, I was unsure if she thought it was best to deny the abuse and neglect or if she thought the living conditions were not detrimental to her children.

Questions

When Children's Protective Services removes a child from their home, they must demonstrate that the children have suffered or are at risk of being abused or neglected.

    1. If a parent is selling illegal drugs out of the home, discuss whether that puts the children at risk of abuse or neglect.

    2. Before reading the next section, how would you approach involuntary clients?

    3. What education or training have you received that specifically prepares you to work with involuntary or coerced clients?

The court placed Blanche on probation after staying in jail for two weeks. She lost possession of her low-income housing because the law stated that if low-income housing is used to sell drugs, the own will be evicted and the property will revert back to the county for the next person on the list waiting for low-income housing. Therefore, she moved in with her brother and sister-in-law. Not Blanche but Nestor called to advise me of her situation and to arrange for a home visit.

Questions

    1. Review your community's policy on selling drugs in low-income housing. What is the policy, and how would it have affected Blanche if she was living in your community?

    2. Discuss your opinion on the policy of eviction for selling drugs. If you had the power to change the policy, explain whether you would change it, and the reasons behind your decision.

As arranged with Nestor, I visited Blanche next at her brother's home. Although she was more verbal during this interview, she continued to appear to be somewhat withdrawn. Blanche often looked to her brother for apparent support. He would answer questions on her behalf or that of the family. It was Nestor who stated that Blanche's relationship with Larry was over and that she was not using drugs any longer, as she would not be allowed in his house if she did. Blanche nodded her consent to these statements. She only gave brief answers to my direct questions.

Nestor was angry that placement of the children in his home was denied and stated his belief that the "state" was again crossing lines in which they had no right to interfere. He believed that protecting and caring for his sister's children was a family responsibility, not a government mandate. The process of client engagement felt stymied. It seemed to me that I was going to have little luck connecting with Blanche, and that Nestor was going to assure that any relationship remained adversarial.

Although I understood Nestor's feelings, I felt as though the negativity was likely having the same effect on Blanche. Blanche adopting what I believed was an attitude of noncompliance could easily lead to the permanent loss of her parental rights. As a foster care worker, I accepted as my role the responsibility of developing and promoting a services plan for Blanche. In order for her to regain custody of her children, it would be necessary for her to accept and cooperate with the plan. I was aware that I was beginning to view Nestor in a less than favorable light and his involvement with the case a liability.

An additional difficulty during this family interview was on a personal level. The family tended to converse with one another in Spanish or a mix of English and Spanish. It took a quick self-assessment to name my discomfort. It would certainly have been insensitive and truly only a futile power move to request them to only speak English during the interview. This was the family's mode of conversation. And if in fact they wished to say things without me hearing them, they could certainly do that when I wasn't around. It was my issue, not theirs.

Questions

The foster care worker noted that during her investigation, the family would speak in a mix of English and Spanish.

   1. **Discuss the impact of language on your ability to conduct an assessment. What steps would you take to overcome that barrier?**

   2. **Because the foster care worker could not understand all of the conversation, how should she have handled the situation at that moment?**

It did appear though, that Nestor and Blanche were not comfortable or willing to provide background information for the assessment. Problem areas were minimized and questions of "family business" were unanswered, leaving questions as to the reasons for the perceived secrecy. Given the family's apparent distrust of the system, and me as an agent thereof, it did not seem that they would warm up to a technique or tool such as a genogram. I did note, however, that the family itself was important from the number of photographs and children's drawings hanging in the home. I utilized these items to focus attention away from the formal interview.

Family photographs, which were hanging on the living room wall, became an opening to ask about the family of origin. They began to open up when I questioned them about people in the photographs or occasions for which they were taken. While describing the subjects in the photographs, Blanche and, to a lesser extent, Nestor began to talk about their background.

Blanche's History

Blanche was the youngest of nine children raised in a two-parent family that traveled seasonally completing seasonal farm work. Nestor was her eldest male sibling. Blanche's father was the lead worker on a local farm, and the family returned to the same farm every year. Blanche described her father as domineering and abusive toward both her mother and toward the children.

Nestor stated that their formal education was difficult to maintain due to their migrant status. Nestor completed a high school equivalency as an adult, however, Blanche's education appeared to have been more limited. Blanche related that she was "slow" in school, eventually dropping out altogether to help take care of children of other families working the farms.

Blanche became pregnant at the age of fifteen. Her parents consented to her marriage to the man by whom she became pregnant. Blanche miscarried the child and her husband left her. Blanche returned to her parents' home. However, she soon became involved with another man who was 20 years her senior. She lived with this man and had her three children by him. She said that he was "undocumented," and he was deported to Mexico during the last pregnancy. Blanche later reported that the deportation concerned weapons charges.

The remainder of Blanche's family relocated permanently to Texas. Nestor and his family settled in the area after the children's father was deported. He had taken on the role as head of the family. Blanche distanced herself from Nestor's family when she became involved with Larry.

Through the Social Services records, I learned that Blanche was receiving what seemed to be sufficient ADC and Food Stamps to meet her children's needs. However, part of the complaint at the time of removal referred to the lack of food and the inadequate living situation. Blanche was questioned about this issue but had no explanation for it. Nestor answered that Larry "stole" her money and that now the family would assure care and responsibility of the children.

Blanche received an evaluation at the County Mental Health agency. The therapist who completed the evaluation was female. Although she was not of Hispanic descent, she had spent a great deal of time immersed in the culture while studying in Mexico. Her cultural insight to the case was probably more valuable than any mental health diagnosis.

Blanche's mental health therapist believed and described to me that her apparent "evasive" demeanor was in line with her familial and cultural norms. The "domineering" influence of Nestor should also be viewed in a cultural light. It began to make sense that Blanche would have allowed a male figure, such as Larry, to take advantage of her home and her finances. The systematic issues present in her community as an "underclass" of the larger society also provided her little opportunity or alternative. She appeared powerless to allow otherwise.

However, the prevailing literature sees these general statements about Mexican families as feeding into stereotypes while dismissing the individual sitting in front of you (Taylor, 1998). Having a foundational understanding of different cultures is a valuable resource, but it should never take the place of listening to the client and working with them to develop a plan that best meets their needs. Practitioners should avoid plans that fit into a prefabricated cultural box. In this case, as part of my assessment, I tried to understand the relationship between Blanche and Nestor, and how that relationship impacted their daily interactions. Unlike the therapist, I had interacted with both Blanche and Nestor. I also wondered how much of their roles were dictated by the big brother protecting his little sister, and I thought about the role of Nestor as head of the extended family (Taylor, 1994; Green 1999). All of those factors were included during my ongoing assessment.

Questions

One of the more difficult challenges when working with clients is understanding another culture. The therapist and the foster care worker did not agree on why Blanche deferred to her brother.

1. Taking all the information you have gathered on the case, discuss why you think Blanche deferred to her brother.

2. Review some of the literature on cultural competency and Mexican culture, and see if the explanations in the literature support or disagree with your position.

My assessment, as well as that of her mental health therapist, directed that individual services for Blanche should focus on issues of substance abuse as well as depression. It was believed that Blanche would have to become empowered and learn to be assertive in order to protect herself from being further taken advantage of. The therapist suggested that Blanche become involved in an outpatient substance abuse treatment program specifically for women.

I understood Nestor's demeanor based on his familial and cultural influences better after receiving this information. It was one of my defining moments as a worker when I realized that judgments and assumptions should never be hastily made. It was not only Nestor's intention to be deemed as the rightful authority in the family but perhaps to assist his sister as well. I also began at that time to more fully realize that expecting conformity to my plans without acknowledging this familial reality could be contrary to the establishment of a helping relationship and of a positive outcome for families.

Child Assessment

Reports from Children's Protective Services indicated that the children displayed little emotion at the time of placement. They readily went with officers and settled in easily to the foster home. Early reports from the foster parent indicated that the baby was somewhat fussy; however, the older two appeared very happy. Both of the younger children appeared to look to Lucy for attention and care.

Early reports from the foster parent described Lucy as a "serious-natured" child. Although she would sometimes play with dolls and toys, she seemed to prefer watching the other children play. She continued to express very little emotion during the initial days of placement. She did seem concerned about her mother's condition and whereabouts and often asked when she could see her.

Lucy and Robert shared a bedroom in the foster home. It was reported that Lucy went to bed in the top bunk each night, but when the children were awakened in the morning, she was in the bottom bunk with her brother. She told the foster mother that she slept with Robert because her brother had been lonely. Lucy also assisted Robert with dressing in the morning and before bed.

The foster parent noted that Lucy attempted to discipline the children. She was quite vigilant in her supervision and became upset when stopped from directing her younger siblings. This information raised concerns regarding Lucy's caretaker role within her family home.

Robert was a delightful child who would often act "foolish" in an attempt to make adults laugh. Robert cried at bedtime during his first days in the foster home. He would not be comforted by anyone except Lucy. Robert enjoyed coloring and watching cartoons. Robert appeared to be of appropriate stature given his chronological age. He displayed no behavioral issues and seemed to become accustomed to the foster home routine within the first week.

Joey was a fussy child and did not sleep through the night. The foster parent stated that he awoke crying throughout the night and was often awake for hours before falling back to sleep. The foster parents believed that Joey wanted Lucy to tend to his needs. They wanted Lucy rested for school, so they did not allow Lucy to get up in the middle of the night to attend to Joey.

Records available from the local clinic indicated that Joey and Robert were significantly behind in their immunizations. A physician had seen neither child since Joey was 6 months old. Both Robert and Joey also presented dental concerns, as their front teeth were badly decayed from what appeared to be "bottle rot."

Joey appeared delayed in his development. His motor skills were more along the line of an 11–12 month old. He was pulling up on furniture, but not yet walking. There were no medical reasons noted for the delays. It was posited that the delays were caused by environmental factors.

Family Interaction

A paraprofessional supervised the family during their visitation time at the agency. Blanche was transported to the visitation by her brother, Nestor. He was required to wait in the lobby for the first half of the visit so that Blanche could have some time alone with her children. This also allowed for some observation of the nuclear family's interactions.

Blanche was very tearful when she initially saw the children. She kissed each and began conversing with them in Spanish. Blanche initially held Joey, and then set him on the floor. She directed Lucy to get him a bottle from the foster parent's diaper bag. She then turned her attention to Robert. Blanche colored in a book with Robert and asked Lucy questions about school and the foster home.

Blanche displayed very little initiative to physically interact with the children and seemed to have difficulty attending to more than one child at a time. Lucy took the lead in entertaining Joey by bringing him various toys. Robert continued to color and also showed his mother his "new trick," which was to somersault. Blanche remained seated in the same place during the first half of the visit.

Nestor participated into the last half-hour of every visit with the children. Lucy immediately ran to him. He took a somewhat background position physically in the room, choosing a single chair near the door. He did, however, seem to become a point of focus for the family. Robert began performing his "tricks" for him and Lucy sat on his lap. Blanche conversed in Spanish with Nestor and paid little attention to the children.

As the visit ended, Joey became fussy and Nestor spoke to Blanche in Spanish. Blanche then arose and picked the child up. She changed his diaper and continued to hold him for the remainder of the visit. Blanche, Lucy, and Robert began to cry when the visit ended. Nestor again spoke to them in Spanish and they calmed somewhat.

The paraprofessional raised the issue of the family speaking Spanish during the visitation. He was concerned that he was to be providing supervision of the visit and could not do so appropriately without understanding the conversations of the family. As there were no concerns that the family would sway the children's testimony, I informed the visitation supervisor to only address issues of physical caretaking and not to be concerned with the language barrier. Not having Spanish-speaking workers was the agency's problem and not the family's.

Questions

Now that the author has presented Blanche's personal history, and before reading further, develop a treatment plan for Blanche and her family.

1. **Develop a list of Blanche's problems and strengths.**

2. **Describe the problems affecting this family.**

3. **Develop goals for the case.**

4. **What steps would you take to demonstrate completion of those goals?**

5. **Describe your roles and responsibilities in the case.**

Intervention

Case Planning

It became clear that for Blanche, intervention might best take place by involving her family system—especially Nestor. From the assessment, and culturally relevant, the "family" for purposes of intervention and support had to be viewed as including the extended family as well as strengths within the community. Although both Nestor and Blanche regarded them as "just more paper," releases of information were signed by Blanche to allow Nestor and his wife to be given case information. I requested that a family meeting be held to discuss case plans. A strength-based, solution-focused approach was utilized to determine desired outcomes and set necessary goals and action steps (Berg, 1994). The family responded well to this approach.

This was decided as a useful approach given what I noted to be a propensity of the family to avoid or minimize problem issues. I also had only a short time frame in which to reach permanency for the children. Solution-focused practice emphasizes solutions rather than dwelling on the problem. Regardless of how or why Blanche found herself in these circumstances, it was going to be necessary to reach certain goals to prove to the court that she was prepared to have her children returned to her care.

Another reason for this approach was the need to have the extended family involved in the case plan. Blanche was less than motivated to make the changes, and possibly unable to avail herself of the strengths in the community over the negative influences individually. The strengths-based model creates and takes advantage of supports within the client's system (Saleeby, 1997). Considering Blanche's isolation from the larger community, and the lack of trust in the system, it would be necessary on a long-term basis to develop natural supports.

Taking into consideration Nestor's "lead" role in the family, I asked him to arrange the place and time for a case-planning meeting. I found this somewhat uncomfortable, as I still believed that Blanche should have taken this responsibility as the parent with whom the agency was mandated to work. However, it seemed to be the natural state for this family, so I tried to mold the usual protocol for case services to fit what this family needed. This fit with the strength-based and solution-focused model (Saleeby, 1997).

Nestor wanted the case-planning meeting held at his home. All parties were in agreement that the eventual goal was to have the "State" out of their lives. That approach was part of Berg's "miracle question" (Berg, 1994). Asking the family how they would like to see themselves in the future was a way for them to say they wanted the state out of their lives. I then asked them what steps we could take for their goal to happen. Although semantics may have differed by the child welfare system, it was in fact my goal as well.

The family wanted Blanche to maintain sobriety, demonstrate appropriate parenting skills, and obtain appropriate housing, with the end goal of her parenting her children. A goal of obtaining current medical and dental treatment for the children was established. Blanche agreed to attend these appointments with the children and the foster parent.

My concerns regarding Lucy's parental role with her siblings was not viewed the same by the family. After I described Lucy's behavior, Blanche denied that Lucy displayed it while in the home, and Nestor believed it was somewhat her responsibility as the eldest child to help care for her younger siblings. They did agree that she would benefit from counseling due to her placement away from her family.

Service Provision

With the plan in writing, the family appeared more positive toward intervention. Blanche stated that she trusted her mental health therapist and wanted to continue to see her for counseling and parenting instruction. She agreed to attend the outpatient substance abuse program the therapist recommended. The family agreed that Lucy should see a children's therapist in the same mental health organization that housed Blanche's therapist. The therapists would work together and develop joint counseling when deemed appropriate by the therapists involved.

The agency would provide financial support to relocate Blanche and her family into a suitable housing arrangement once she successfully completed the treatment goals. Nestor had been helping to remodel the house next to his for his landlord. As the owner was a friend and was aware of Blanche's situation, he was willing to allow her to move into the home for the same rent she paid for the smaller home she had when the children were removed.

The family stated that their most pressing need was to have the children placed with them. The reasons for the denial of placement were again discussed. However, the visitations moved to Nester's home, rather than at the social services office.

The most dominant strength on which Blanche had to draw appeared to be that of her extended family and community, especially Nestor. He offered to assist with transportation for Blanche to necessary services. The family would have visitation with the children two times a week at Nestor's home during this time. Nestor and his wife would also allow Blanche to remain in their home while she was in treatment.

It appeared as though engagement with Blanche was occurring vicariously through a relationship with Nestor. Trust was built with Nestor by respecting his role within the family and by taking a strength-based approach. Whether it was by trust of or force from her brother, Blanche in turn began to cooperate with services.

Progress

Blanche initially attended her counseling and women's group. The substance abuse therapist indicated that while she was attending scheduled appointments, she appeared to be minimizing her history of substance use. She continued to blame Larry for her situation and claimed that she had only occasionally used drugs in the past.

Blanche was present for visitations with her children. However, she continued to be relatively inactive with them, as reported by the paraprofessional supervising the visit. She was instructed that she was to provide the direct care to the children, rather than allowing Lucy or Nestor to do it. Although she often failed to take action independently, she did respond well to redirection by the paraprofessional or Nestor.

During this same time, Lucy began to withdraw from her parenting role at the foster home. It was noted that she was beginning to display more emotions from all realms of the spectrum. She laughed more readily, and displayed anger more often.

However, these were all felt to be within normal limits. Most encouraging was that it appeared she was beginning to enjoy acting like a child.

Robert began to have his dental issues managed and Joey received medical attention including immunizations. Joey received developmental assessments and early childhood program referrals to fully investigate Joey's perceived delays.

By the time the children had been in care six weeks, Blanche tested positive for cocaine during a random drug screening at her substance abuse treatment program. She denied that she had used any drugs and submitted to another test. Her attendance at scheduled appointments and visitation also began to drop during this time, possibly indicating a relapse. By the time her second drug screen returned with a positive result for cocaine, she had moved out of her brother's home without warning and her whereabouts were unknown for much of the time.

Nestor immediately informed the agency about Blanche's disappearance. He was sure that she was staying with various friends in the community, but he was also sure that she would not return to his home if she was again using drugs.

When Blanche could be located, Nestor provided her transportation to appointments for substance abuse treatment. An early childhood parenting program was arranged to teach Blanche parenting techniques during visitation with her children. This program used paraprofessionals to demonstrate hands-on techniques with the parent in their own home. This program was offered to Blanche in Nestor's home. Therefore, if Blanche "no-showed" a visitation, Nestor and his family had the advantage of the service as well.

Through the implementation of services to assist Blanche, Nestor seemed to glean some insight as well. He noted that he had learned several new techniques for discipline and was using them with his own children. His demeanor toward the case, and me as the worker, seemed to lighten. He stated that he believed his sister could gain assistance if she would only take advantage of the services offered.

I began to discuss with Nestor the concept of relapse. It is expected that a client in recovery from substance abuse may relapse (Johnson, 2004). It is especially of concern in the isolated environmental situation such as the one in which Blanche was residing. There was little else to occupy her time or fill the void the drugs once occupied. This coupled with her depression made relapse very probable.

As noted under engagement, child welfare services depends on reengaging the client quickly. The counter toward permanency planning remains in play regardless of the reality of a relapse. Nestor was asked to encourage Blanche to contact her therapist or myself. However, Blanche remained out of contact for several weeks.

Questions

1. From a review of the professional literature of substance abuse, discuss the concept of relapse and the role it plays in treatment planning.

2. There is inherent conflict between the concept of relapse and the goal of providing permanency for children. When children are in foster care, how many relapses (and over what period of time) can a parent have before you decide that

the length of time in foster care is harming the children? Discuss your personal opinion and then review whether the professional literature supports your position.

Case Crisis

The children had been in foster care for approximately three months when I received a call during the night from the Children's Protective Services "on call" worker. The worker had been called to the hospital earlier in the evening and was informed that the foster parent had brought Joey to the emergency room that evening. Joey was lethargic and appeared ill. Tests were run and it was determined that Joey suffered a skull fracture and was bleeding around the brain. Joey died shortly after his arrival at the hospital.

A CPS worker investigating Joey's death placed Lucy and Robert in a different foster home. The CPS worker informed the uncle and me of Joey's death, but no one knew where Blanche was staying.

Case Management Issues

A case meeting brought the foster care workers, staff and supervisors, foster home licensing, and Children's Protective Services together the next day. Because this case affected a large bureaucracy, it was necessary to reduce the event into writing so that the administrators within the organization had the facts available. While discussing those facts and trying to comprehend the whole situation, the fact that Joey's death evoked such a business-like discussion left me with an overarching sense of surrealism.

I was lucid to the fact that a family was mourning and would be looking for, and deserving, answers. There was also the sick ironic realization that the very purpose of the agency's intervention with the family was to protect Joey from possible harm, and he had in fact been placed in harm's way. I was dreading the inevitable confrontation with this family for whom I would have no possible adequate response.

During the case discussion in supervision, I learned that the foster mother had left the children in the care of her adult nephew. This young man was not living in the home and was not part of the license. He was asked to baby-sit the children while his aunt went shopping. When she returned, she found the baby ill in the crib. The other children were sitting quietly watching a movie.

The nephew initially denied that he had any knowledge of how the skull fracture could have occurred. He later stated that he and the children were in the front yard during the afternoon. Lucy and Robert were by the side of the house on a swing set and Joey was on the front steps. He claimed that he turned his back for a minute to attend to the girls when Joey fell down the concrete steps, hitting his head on the cement walk.

The foster parent's nephew stated that he did not see any injuries and that the child seemed fine. He stated that the baby vomited and seemed sleepy so he put him in his crib.

The Children's Protective Services investigator stated that the doctors were suspicious of the story, as there were no outward scrapes or bruises to indicate that the child had hit concrete. They also seemed to believe that there had to be more force than would be generated from a fall down the steps to cause such an injury.

There were no other indications of abuse or neglect to any of the children in the home. The only other children in the home at the time of the injury were Lucy and Robert. Neither of them was able to provide any initial information to investigators at the hospital. Lucy simply stated, "Joey got real sick," and that "Joey not alive anymore."

I remembered at the case meeting that Nestor and his wife knew of the child's death. As word of the tragedy spread through the community, Blanche heard the news and returned to Nestor's home. It was time for someone to talk to the family.

Within the agency, Joey's death was the epitome of everyone's "worst nightmare." Support was found through coworkers who, although not having experienced the same situation, could imagine the feelings of grief, confusion, and fear that accompany such a tragedy. There was an overall sense of worry throughout the agency as assumptions were made regarding lawsuits and how the story would be played out in the media. A first-line supervisor who acted as buffer between the seemingly emotionless mandates of the upper administration and the harsh realities of direct involvement with the family provided direction.

Agency Investigation

It was necessary for the agency to investigate the circumstances surrounding the death. To do this, Joey's case file was confiscated, as was the foster home file. This was done in such a manner that it was impossible to not feel as if the work was being questioned or workers being personally blamed. This feeling was further established when the files were returned with a statement that it had been determined that all policies had been followed and documented in the case files. The administration noted that this would assist the agency and individual workers to address any lawsuits.

It was understood that these issues would have had to have been addressed. However, on a personal level this knowledge was of no help in alleviating any of the anxiety that I experienced in the days after Joey's death. As the primary caseworker, I felt the impact on a more personal level. I felt as though I was vacillating between shock and horror. The most forefront thing on my mind was that I had denied a relative placement in favor of licensed foster care, and believed I had done so in the children's best interests. I also grieved for the child. This was a child I knew well, cared about, and was responsible for. Initially the emotions were almost overwhelming.

Supervision was utilized formally and informally during this time to assure that my casework functions were being covered. Every decision made in a child welfare case can affect many lives for years. Immediately following this tragedy, the enormity of these decisions became abundantly clear, and it became very difficult for me to make independent decisions on this or any other case. In all cases, we use case supervision to review all contingencies and ensure that there is clear decision making. When a child dies, a special committee that includes people not involved in the case meets in order to bring objectivity to the process.

We all presumed that Nestor would be adamant that his niece and nephew live with him following this incident. I found it very difficult to rationalize reasons for denial at that time. In reassessing this request in supervision, the initial home study was drawn on. Issues that caused the denial were brought out. The supervisor questioned whether these situations described had changed since the writing of the study, thereby making the home safe and acceptable for placement of the children. Since they had not, the placement could not be approved, regardless of the death of Joey. Supervision was incredibly helpful in separating issues during this time.

Supervisor oversight and assurance of appropriate casework and decision making on this and other cases helped me eventually regain confidence to continue a career in the child welfare field. It was also the first-line supervisors who were cognizant of the emotional toll this situation took on direct care workers. While managing the crisis within the Raney family, and the accompanying personal issues, thirty other children on my caseload demanded—and deserved—attention.

Initially, weighing the fear of facing this family, and the onslaught of the anger and blame they were likely to display, with the realization that assisting and supporting families through this type of situation was part of the profession, was overwhelmingly difficult. Although my supervisor suggested having another worker fill in for a while, I deemed it a moral obligation to contact the family and bring the children to Nestor's home for an extended visit immediately. It had become clear that family was a source of strength for them; therefore, this had to be honored.

Questions

The death of a child is a horrifying event for the parents, relatives, friends, and the professionals involved with the case. It is also an event that can haunt siblings for life. Given the nature of the death and the number of people it affected, please respond to the following questions.

    1. Examine the literature on childhood trauma. See how the literature discusses this type of event. Based on your examination, describe the different types of childhood trauma and the emotional and behavioral affects it can have on Lucy and Robert.

2. **Before their placement in foster care, Lucy appeared to be the primary caretaker of Joey. How does the literature discuss this phenomenon? Is Lucy's grief more like a sibling or a parent?**

3. **You have a detailed psychosocial history of Joey's mother, Blanche. Based on your assessment and treatment plan, how will the death of Joey affect her ability to complete the treatment plan in order to gain custody of her other two children? How would you engage Blanche in therapy?**

4. **Examine the literature on trauma to social workers. Describe the emotional and behavioral affects it can have on professionals.**

5. **What steps should the agency take to ensure the mental health of its workers in the aftermath of a child on their caseload dying?**

Telling the Family

As expected, Nestor was verbally aggressive over the telephone, stating that the "state" had killed Joey, who would still be alive if the children were in his care. He gave the phone to his wife, who agreed to have the children brought to the home that morning for a visit.

The drive to and arrival at Nestor's home was a time of anxiety. I began to prepare myself for the onslaught of anger. Although there had never been a sense of physical danger at the home in the past, my supervisor and I discussed my safety before the home visit.

Upon arrival, it was clear that the news had spread throughout the community. Neighbors had sent food and many "kin" folk were gathered at the house. Blanche was absent, having left the previous evening to stay with friends. Nestor came from the house to the car. The amazing strength embodied by human beings was then evidenced as Nestor apologized for his earlier anger and tears, stating that, "We know this isn't your fault. You cared about him too."

Expressing grief and tears with the client family may not be a lauded therapeutic technique, but there are times that professionalism gives way to reality and humanness. It was at that moment that I believe I was, to a greater extent, accepted by the family as I spent the afternoon with them listening, talking, and crying. There was a point of concurrence between the "professional" and the family. Everyone could agree that the tragedy should never have occurred, and no one could ignore the real loss and sorrow within the room.

It seems that the willingness to allow the family to see (or perhaps the lack of ability to prevent it) that Joey's death was indeed deeply felt on a personal level built a level of trust and rapport that I would have thought unimaginable under the circumstances. The family received all of the information provided by the foster parent's nephew regarding the injury Joey sustained. They were also informed that the police and the foster home licensing unit were investigating the situation. Nestor and his family were offered counseling. The family declined this service, stating that they would speak with their priest if they felt the need.

Nestor stated that Joey was now "in God's hands" and that he would be their angel. The family's priest was at the home and it was learned that the family was making arrangements for a funeral when additional family members arrived from Texas. It became clear that religion played an important role in Nestor's family and had been overlooked in earlier assessments. Later discussions revealed that while Blanche had fallen away from the church years before, she did have all of her children baptized. Nestor's family attended mass regularly in the neighborhood Catholic church. The fact that Joey was baptized brought some comfort to Nestor.

As expected, Nestor again asked for placement of Lucy and Robert. Since the health and safety of the children was the reason for his denial, we could not say that he would have done worse. Nestor wanted the children safe and with him.

I went over the reason again for his denial. Nestor was told that it was a truly agonizing denial. He accepted this, but asked for assistance in meeting with the prosecuting attorney. Nestor did not want his sister or the rest of his family to know, but he was not accepting the story given by the foster parent's nephew. He, however, did not believe that the prosecutor would meet with him without a presence from the child welfare agency.

Later that week I arranged a meeting with the prosecuting attorney. He explained to Nestor that there was no evidence at this point to arrest any suspect for murder. There was insufficient evidence to confirm or refute the claim of the foster parent's nephew that the child's fall was an accident. Neither evidence from the medical examiner nor the police had been sufficient to determine a definite cause for the injury. Nestor was assured that there would be a continuing investigation.

Lucy and Robert spent extended time with the family before and during the funeral. Their new foster parents also attended the funeral at the request of the family. Nestor did not ask the first foster parents to attend the funeral.

Reassessment

Blanche attended one individual therapy session following Joey's death. The therapist was concerned with her presentation, stating that she was beginning to talk about suicidal ideation. The therapist, after assessment, did not believe that she was an active suicide threat. However, she gained Blanche's permission to share the concern with Nestor and me.

During this time, the children continued in foster care placement. Visitation was maintained with the mother and relatives, and Lucy continued in therapy. According to the new foster parents, Robert displayed no behavior problems and seemed to fit in well in the home. While he often cried when visitation with the relatives was concluded, he appeared to be coping with the additional placement change. Lucy, on the other hand, began to have severe behavioral problems at this time.

Following the death of her sibling, and subsequent placement in a new foster home, Lucy's personality and affect changed. The new foster parent described Lucy as unpredictable. She seemed afraid of most adults and rarely laughed. She became very clingy with her uncle and the caseworker, but was distant to her mother and foster mother. She was usually sullen and withdrawn, yet would at times become extremely angry, throwing tantrums that resulted in harm to property and other children. It was also interesting to note that Lucy no longer attempted to provide the "mother" role for Robert. Lucy would have nighttime enuresis and had difficulty sleeping. She vacillated between refusing to eat and binge eating.

Both Lucy and Robert appeared to not only be grieving for their brother, about whom they did not speak without provocation, but also for their former foster mother, about whom they asked often. It appeared that there was a bond established between the foster mother and the children during their stay in her home. The hasty removal and placement along with the tragedy of Joey's death and the underlying separation from the biological parent was having an evident impact, especially on Lucy.

Information from her kindergarten teacher claimed the same behaviors were displayed in school as in the foster home. At times Lucy would refuse to play with other children and simply sit by herself appearing "spaced out," as the teacher referred to it. Other times she would decide that she wanted to play with something another child had and aggressively take the toy, resulting in an altercation. During structured work times Lucy fared better. She was often able to pay attention and seemed to regain some of her "old" personality when called on by the teacher.

The foster parent reported an incident in which Lucy was playing dolls with another child in the home. Lucy threw the doll onto the floor telling it to "Shut up! You not alive no more!" When approached by the foster parent she ran crying to her bedroom and refused to talk about it.

Treatment

Therapy for Lucy

Lucy continued to have weekly appointments with her therapist during this time. The therapist utilized play therapy with her young clients, including Lucy. She stated that Lucy was very matter-of-fact in discussing that her brother had died; however, she would not discuss the issue at any greater depth. Her play had become indicative of the trauma she was experiencing.

Play therapy was the preferred mode of therapy for Lucy due to her young age and the circumstances affecting her young life. Through her actions, it appeared that she was displaying turmoil within her psyche that she was unequipped to handle on a verbal or even very functional level. From prior assessment, it was assumed that as Lucy considered herself responsible for her siblings, the death of one of them "under her watch" was causing extreme trauma. Perhaps this trauma increased further when she began to relinquish her parental role during her foster home placement.

Before her brother's death, her play often imitated "caretaking" themes. After that time, her play was more in line with the angry demeanor she was expressing at school. She would smash clay or throw items. Her drawings showed Lucy or her Mom seemingly suspended in the air with no mouth or limbs.

The therapist, as well as the police and other investigation personnel, believed that Lucy likely witnessed whatever action led to the injury and death of Joey. The lack of a mouth in her drawing led the therapist to wonder if she was threatened to not tell what she saw in the foster home that day or if she was keeping a "secret" from some other time. While interested in the discovery of any information Lucy might be able to provide, her therapist focused on her needs and the treatment was nondirected. It determined that Lucy was exhibiting symptoms of Post Traumatic Stress Disorder. She was attempting to manage her own guilt in the situation while grieving the losses in her life.

Lucy was displaying a lack of trust and attachment with most adults at that time. She had certainly suffered the loss of important people in her life, as well as possibly witnessing the fatal injury of her sibling by a trusted adult. Lucy had "lost" her mother, their community, way of life, her sibling, and a foster mother to whom she had formed a quick attachment.

Intervention for Lucy was to include weekly play therapy and ongoing team meetings between the foster parent, caseworker, therapist, and hopefully Blanche. It was the goal of therapy for Lucy to gain mastery of the trauma involved with Joey's death and return to pre-trauma functioning. It was also hoped that the previous goals of boundary establishment would take place. A secondary goal of the treatment team was for Lucy to be able to provide information regarding Joey's death.

Goals Redefined

Engaging Blanche in Lucy's treatment was unsuccessful. Blanche was unable to reestablish work toward her previously established goals. Meeting with Blanche became difficult, as she would fail to appear for scheduled appointments. Nestor, therefore, replaced Blanche on Lucy's treatment team.

The mother's substance use increased following the death of Joey. Blanche's emotional condition continued to spiral. She again left Nestor's home and was feared to be heavily involved in drug use. Nestor seemed angry with his sister for "running away" and "choosing" drugs over her children. Blanche was reportedly staying with a new male friend. Nestor reported knowledge that they were staying at a known drug house. Service providers left messages for Blanche with Nestor without success. Given her level of chronic and situational depression, they were concerned that she might overdose.

Nestor again contacted the agency within a week of Blanche's disappearance. He reported that his mother had called from Texas. Blanche had appeared on her doorstep asking for help. Apparently Blanche decided to return to Texas with family who had come for the funeral. Nestor stated that he believed Blanche would remain in Texas and that she would be taken care of there. This seemed to relieve Nestor and his anger regarding Blanche subsided.

I attempted to contact Blanche in Texas to offer to assist her in finding services in that state, but she never replied to my letters. She failed to appear at any of the further court proceedings in the juvenile court, although her attorney was able to report contact with his client and verify her whereabouts in Texas.

The case plan for reunification with Blanche was no longer a viable option. Without the availability of a relative placement, the case plan was destined to move toward termination of parental rights.

Nestor and his wife became very involved in therapy with Lucy. They were able to bring suggestions from the therapist into their visitation. Collateral therapeutic work was undertaken between the therapist and adult caretakers (foster parent and Nestor) in an attempt to effectively handle Lucy's tantrums and work toward reestablishing a role for her in the family system. One tactic employed involved Lucy spending one-on-one time with the foster mother preparing dinner. The actual meal was prepared by the foster parent, while Lucy prepared a special dessert. It was believed that this gave her a role as a sibling rather than a primary caretaker. It also provided Lucy with individual attention. She seemed to speak more freely while she was involved in the activity.

Lucy progressed in therapy. Although she continued to display behavioral issues, her tantrums began to decrease in frequency and intensity. Therapy reports began to indicate that stability and permanence was going to be an important goal for Lucy. The child understood that she would not be returning to her mother and was questioning where she belonged.

Reports received from Lucy's school and therapist indicated that Nestor was more involved than many parents in the child's progress. Even the foster parents questioned the agency's decision to not place the children with his family.

Permanency Goal

This situation caused a turning point in the case planning. It had been a rather cavalier attitude (but the prevailing one at the time) that once a relative was denied placement, the option was closed. The thought of the children losing these relatives, especially in light of their other losses, was unimaginable. I was certain, as was the child's therapist, that Lucy would be devastated by such a decision. Given the situation in this case, I discussed with my supervisor the idea of placing Lucy and Robert with their uncle.

Recommending placement of children with relatives who had prior Children's Protective Services history was a difficult step to take. By all appearances, it seemed that this family should be given the benefit of growth and change. Yet if a child was hurt in this home in which prior abuse was documented, there would be no sufficient excuse for the decision. There was no concern by any of the service providers with Nestor's care of his, or Blanche's, children. The participation of the relatives with services and the positive reports received from providers rekindled the idea of Nestor having custody of the children.

Based largely on these positive provider reports, it was decided that if the other barriers toward placement were overcome, namely housing and income, the placement would be approved. This illuminated a great gap in service provision. Licensed foster parents received a daily stipend or per diem to care for children, but there was no substantial funding for assisting relative or "kinship" care providers.

Nestor was told about the possible placement. Within a week and as the case neared six months out of home, Nestor and his wife appeared at the social services office. Nestor stated that his landlord was allowing him to "swap" houses. Nestor and his family were going to be allowed to move into the larger house he had originally planned for Blanche. This would provide sufficient space for Robert and Lucy. Nestor's wife had taken a part-time job to bring more income into the home. Although the income would still be tight, it appeared that financial obligations would be met. Nestor also provided a written reference letter from his priest offering any assistance the church could provide to assist Nestor's family in caring for his niece and nephew. After witnessing the family and community come together over the past six months, no one had reason to believe that the family would be incapable of caring for Robert and Lucy. Upon their move to a larger home, the children were placed with them.

Case Termination

The foster care case remained open while the children received supervision in their relatives' care. The court case and social services involvement could not close until a legal resolution or permanency plan was in place for the children. The parental rights of Blanche were still intact, although she had no contact with the children or plans to reunify.

Given the children's age, the agency decided to petition the court for termination of parental rights. That would free the children for adoption. The adoptive parents would have been eligible for an adoption subsidy from the state. This payment would have been equal to the foster care payment rate and would be of great assistance if the relatives adopted.

Nestor and his family instead asked for a guardianship to be established. Even though they were aware that this would not give them the financial benefits of adoption, they chose to not have further investigations into their home by an adoption worker. It was not unusual in their family and culture for relatives to care for one another's children when needed. There was no stigma with the children in relative care. They also did not want to make Blanche's situation worse with a termination and adoption, as this meant Blanche would no longer be a mother.

Guardianship was not a preferred permanency plan for children of this age, especially in cases where it appeared clear that the parent was not going to make any efforts toward reunification. Playing into the preferential view of termination may have been the underlying knowledge that adoption numbers can equate to staffing for the agency. Adoption counts are used as part of the agency and director performance evaluation. There is no financial or staffing incentive to the agency for guardianships.

The final decision regarding the agency's recommendation for permanency of Lucy and Robert occurred at a case staffing. From previous experience, a push from supervision toward the permanency plan of termination and adoption was expected, but did not occur. It was possible that Nestor and his family had established their ability to provide for their relatives without further intervention. It also seemed that the agency was eager to close these cases and move on. In either case, the guardianship of Lucy and Robert with Nestor's family was established.

Questions

1. **Why did Nestor want guardianship for the two children?**

2. **The agency decided to place the children with Nestor under a guardianship agreement and not an adoption. If the goal is permanency, discuss what effect guardianship had on that goal.**

The family was able to establish a payments assistance grant for the children consisting of approximately one hundred dollars per month for each child. They also received Medicaid for the children, which allowed them to continue Lucy's therapy. The court closed the foster care case regarding Lucy and Robert within eight months of their original placement in foster care.

Once the court dismisses a foster care case and services by the agency are closed, there is no legal basis for continued involvement. A worker may remain involved individually, keeping in mind that families are not always welcoming of a visit from their previous foster care worker. Contact after the close of a case might be seen as an intrusion or a "set-up."

Nestor did maintain contact with me for the first two months of the guardianship. He reported that Lucy continued in therapy and was settling in much better at home. Her behavior at school had also stabilized. While not yet her "old self," she was making progress. Shortly thereafter, Nestor arranged (with the help of his priest) to relocate the children and his family to Texas to be near Blanche and their other relatives. There was no further contact from them after the move.

Evaluation of Practice

Strangely enough, raw data would indicate a very successful intervention for Robert and Lucy. The children reached permanence well within the established 12-month period prescribed by policy. A qualitative evaluation of the case continues to be more difficult and questionable even many years later.

The system failed this family on many levels from the beginning of the case. The children were removed from their familiar community and placed outside of their cultural identity. There were not enough resources, or perhaps insight, available to assist the relatives in obtaining placement of the children within this realm. The strengths of the family were underestimated and only became clear when they asserted them beyond what was "expected." This was not only a system failure, but also a personal one for me as the primary caseworker.

Although in this case Nestor's intervention had positive results, there are often cases in which relatives are likely incapable of presenting these types of strengths.

The lack of resources for relative or kinship placement continues to be a real barrier for such placements for many families. In many regions, unless the relatives of at-risk children can become licensed through the state, they cannot receive stipends equal (or even close) to those received by a foster home. Guardianships in many states are unsubsidized, leaving the same dichotomous situation between that permanency option and adoption. There is an overall push toward relative or kinship placement that was not evident in the child welfare field when this case was open. There now exist several in-home and community-based services that can be utilized to support these placements. This would have been an invaluable tool for Blanche's family.

Another failure in the system is the lack of support available to the foster parent following the death of a child in their care. Immediately following the child's death, a licensing investigation begins in addition to the standard police investigation. In this type of situation, the agency worker who licensed the home and had been the foster family's ongoing support person now becomes an adversary as part of the investigation team. Workers from the agency cannot discuss the issue with the foster parent. In Joey's case, the person we had trusted with the children was ostracized while her family was under suspicion. It was clear that the agency attempted to distance itself from her home. She was provided the number for a foster parent advocacy group, but no one checked whether she ever made contact. It was rumored that she was hospitalized shortly thereafter with both medical and mental health issues.

Although Blanche did not respond as strongly as Nestor to the strength-based/solution-focused approach, it did appear to be successful in her family's case. Progress and goal attainment was achieved at some level. This did appear to be a culturally sensitive approach with this family, considering the dynamics. Accepting and depending on these strengths as sufficient to care for their own issues seemed central to the progress this family made. It was an important realization that it was the family who taught me to value this strength. I had failed to recognize, or perhaps trust, it initially.

Lucy never presented any information regarding Joey's death that led to any further investigation. No one was criminally charged with the death. The family never sought to sue the agency or foster parent for the child's death. The local newspaper articles focused on the criminal investigation and prosecutor's office, as these were the concerns the family brought to them. The agency remained overlooked and silent; there was nothing of relevance for them to add.

Personally, it remains impossible not to posit that if I had originally placed the children with Nestor, Joey might still be alive. That leads me to further hypothesize that if that had occurred, Blanche might have been able to manage a successful recovery and regain custody of her children. It is certain that Lucy would not have suffered such severe trauma in that case. These hypothetical situations cannot, of course, be answered, or change the outcome of this case. As a professional, I find it imperative to look for lessons learned. Then, I can focus future efforts on diligence and use those lessons to assist other families.

Questions

1. What are the permanency guidelines in your state? How long can a child stay in foster care before you have to return the child home, or terminate the parent's parental rights?

2. What type of funding do foster parents receive? Is that funding available for relative and fictive placements?

3. What is the foster care and adoption corporal punishment policy in your state? Explain your reasons for supporting the policy or wanting the policy changed.

4. What was the rational for not placing the children with Nestor? How would the policy in your state have affected that decision?

5. Overall, what is your opinion of the work performed in this case? As always, refer to the professional literature, practice evidence, your experience, and the experience of student-colleagues when developing your opinion.

6. What did this case demonstrate that you could use in other practice settings? List the most important things you learned and how you can use these in your practice career.

Bibliography

Berg, I. K. (1994). *Family-based services: A solution-focused approach.* New York: W. W. Norton & Company.

Green, J. W. (1999). *Cultural awareness in the human service: A multi-ethnic approach.* Boston: Allyn and Bacon.

Johnson, J. L. (2004). *Fundamentals of substance abuse practice.* Pacific Grove, CA: Brooks/Cole.

Miller, T. L. (1999). Permanency planning hearings. Child protective proceedings benchbook: A guide to abuse and neglect cases [on-line]. Available: http://www.courts.mi.gov/mji/resources/cppbook/chapter17.pdf.

Saleeby, D. (ed.). (1997). *The strengths perspective in social work practice.* New York: Longman.

Taylor, R. L. (e4d.). (1998). *Minority families in the United States: A multicultural perspective* (2nd ed.). Englewood Cliffs, NJ: Prentice Hall.

3

Lost in a Foreign Land

George Grant, Jr.

Introduction

Foster care is frequently an umbrella expression that includes Children's Protective Services, residential care, adoption, family preservation, and a variety of actual foster care programs. However, foster care can also include refugee or unaccompanied minor programs. This last type of foster care provides some unique challenges and skills in order to work effectively with this population. Working with people from countries other than the United States requires an understanding of their race, culture, gender, and religion. Practitioners should consider how those identities function and manifest themselves in a foreign environment, where their usual interactions are no longer acceptable and encouraged. How people foreign to those customs, beliefs, and values understand and respond to those differences also affects clients. This case focuses on many of the aforementioned issues. It centers on a teenager refugee living in the United States, dealing with new customs and values, while experiencing separation and loss, abandonment, neglect, and abuse from the people and environment that he understands. At the same time, this teenager is moving through the awkward stages of adolescence.

The central figure in this case, Omar, was in need of support, advocacy, and counseling services. The foster care agency provided the first two things, but needed someone to provide the counseling. I had experience working with refugee children and had performed contract work with the agency in the past. Therefore, they contacted me regarding Omar, a seventeen-year-old male of African decent living in foster care. Omar had gotten into several fights, and the parents of those teenagers asked the prosecutor to arrest him. The prosecutor told the foster care agency that

Omar would go to jail if he got into another fight. Since Omar was not a United States citizen, the prosecutor said that Omar would stay in jail until his eighteenth birthday. He would then petition the Immigration and Nationalization Service (INS) to have Omar deported back to Africa.

This case depicts an adolescent refugee who struggled to make sense of a new land, a new culture, and the discrimination it brought. The adjustment process was confounded by the years of grief, loss, abandonment, and abuse that played a significant role in his reality for the majority of his life.

The initial referral from the foster care agency requested that I address the issue of Omar fighting in school. At the time of the referral, Omar was serving a five-day suspension from high school for fighting. Omar's suspension commenced on a Monday, and the foster care worker contacted me the following day. I scheduled an appointment with Omar and the foster mother for Wednesday morning.

Foster Care Involvement

Omar entered the United States with his paternal uncle. The INS granted him refugee status after his uncle abandoned him. The INS made unsuccessful attempts to look for his uncle or any other relative to provide for his care. Desiring to keep Omar in the area, the INS contracted with a local child welfare agency that provided foster care services. That agency did not have a federal contract to place refugee children, but had experience placing older children in foster care and in finding adoptive homes for children from outside of the United States. The foster care agency had a limited number of foster home placements, but found a family that had experience with older special needs children.

The foster care agency provided traditional foster care, adoption, and independent living programs. The state government contracted with them to provide foster care and adoptive services, and the agency assigned a foster care worker to the case. The worker first met with Omar at the local INS office. After explaining her role and telling him about foster care, she contacted the foster home for an emergency placement.

A select few families agree to accept emergency placements with little or no notice. Some agencies train a certain number of foster families to take children with a variety of behavioral and emotional needs. Not all families can effectively handle all types of children, which makes the family assessment crucial to selecting a successful match. In more long-term foster care, the family is given time to talk to the foster care worker, to review the child's file, and meet the child. This is not an option with emergency placements.

The Hawkins's foster home agreed to accept him as an emergency placement. The foster care worker explained to Omar the placement and the types of services and support he would receive in foster care. The foster care worker would continue to meet with Omar and the Hawkins's every two weeks thereafter. Upon placement, the worker arranged a medical and dental examination for Omar and enrolled him in the local high school.

Questions

1. Research how the INS designates children as refugees. What are the eligibility requirements? How many children are allowed in the United States each year? What states are refugee children placed in?

2. Once children are placed in the United States, what legal rights do they have? Consider things like, can they work? If they work, do they pay social security? Can they attend school and go to college? Must they leave the county by a certain time?

The Therapist

The foster care worker referred the case to me to address Omar's fighting in school. The worker wanted Omar to receive therapy from an African-American male therapist. She felt it was imperative to address the issue expediently and believed that configuration would make him less resistant to therapy. She hoped that would allow Omar to show some progress before he returned to school. Omar's foster care worker hoped that breaking down barriers would demonstrate that Omar was making progress. If progress was observable, it might reduce the chance of the prosecutor following through with the arrest warrant.

At the time I accepted the case I had worked in child welfare for a number of years before starting contract work. I specialized in working with some of the more difficult families and children cases, in which agencies had been struggling to produce positive results. As part of that work, I had previous experience working with refugee children from ten different countries.

The preliminary information came to me through a telephone referral from the foster care worker. My assessment begins at the point of the referral. Some therapists choose to begin a case cold, so as not to bias their initial assessment. They believe that having the information before meeting with the client will form preconceptions of the client and his or her problems. They further believe that the therapist will design the intervention before the client can tell his or her story. My philosophy runs contrary to this practice. I attempt to gather all the available information in order to assist me in formulating questions, listening for gaps in the discussion, and ensuring that I am assessing all the areas that could affect the client's life.

Question

When a worker can make a targeted referral, there is a rationale behind why that person is selected. The foster care worker referred the case to the author because they had a good working relationship, he had experience working with refugee children, she liked the quality of his work, and he was an African American. Because of his race and gender, she thought that Omar might respond to therapy faster. Professionals are matched to clients by religion, personal experiences, shared life experiences, age, geographic location, and personality traits.

1. Review the professional literature and develop positions on the benefits and disadvantages of matching professionals to clients.

Assessment: Foster Mother

The foster mother and Omar came to my office on that Wednesday morning. I met with the foster mother alone to get some background on the foster home, Omar's adjustment to his placement, and any insight the foster mother could provide about the fighting at school. The foster care worker needed to meet with Omar, so they met in my conference room while the foster mother and I talked in my office.

Omar had been living in the foster home just over 40 days when the foster care worker talked to me about providing therapy. The foster mother, Mrs. Hawkins, thought that Omar had adjusted to living in the United States and to their home. He understood the house rules and expectations, and he got along with their family and their few remaining friends. Mrs. Hawkins remarked that she and her husband enjoyed having him around the house. They believed he was happy to be living in the United States. Although he had talked little about his past, most of the stories he told were not of happy memories. He expressed his gratitude to them for letting him live in their home, and was always willing to help with any project.

Mrs. Hawkins said that Omar was not resistant to the foster home placement. He showed them respect and complied with their rules. He assisted around the house and enjoyed spending time with the entire family. The Hawkins's two adult sons came to the house to visit with Omar, and they took him on outings. Mr. and Mrs. Hawkins made a concerted effort to involve Omar with people within his chronological peer group.

The foster mother told me about their efforts to introduce him to some of the teenagers in their neighborhood. However, most of the parents of the teenagers were not supportive of Omar living in the community, and they had concerns about their children interacting with him. It became clear to the Hawkins's that their social contacts in the neighborhood were retreating. They found fewer invitations to parties and community events in the short time Omar had lived in their home. Most of their neighbors and friends stopped calling and visiting. They had had foster children in their home in the past, but he was the first black child in the neighborhood.

During my assessment with Mrs. Hawkins, I found her discussion about Omar's journey to the United States consistent with other discussions about refugee children. Mrs. Hawkins saw Omar's journey as a series of events or developmental milestones. She classified parts of his life as "good" and others as "horrifying." She believed that the past mistreatment he received no longer consumed him. She saw his new life as a positive because he was no longer in those horrible places (Bolea, Grant, Burgess, & Plasa, 2003). As I listened to Mrs. Hawkins, I wondered how Omar would see his life. In most of my work with refugees, it was more likely that Omar would see his life as one continuous story rather than as a series of milestones (Bolea, Grant, Burgess, & Plasa, 2003).

An essential part of working with someone is understanding the cultural reference in which he views his life (Feagin & Feagin, 1999). We all have a way of socially constructing our lives so that we can make sense of the world around us (Berger & Luckmann, 1972). It does not matter how wonderful or difficult our life is; we all must understand our place in the world.

Omar's Adjustment

During our conversation, the foster mother offered two areas of possible concerns. From a cultural standpoint, Omar had a difficult time understanding why the foster father would adhere to the wishes of his wife. It confused him that the foster father did not behave in the male dominant role to which Omar was accustomed. The second area of concern involved the amount of time the family spent together. He was used to being isolated from the other people in his home, and he found it difficult to adjust to all the comings and goings in the foster home. The foster mother stated that he spent hours alone in his room sitting on his bed with his legs crossed. He had a television and radio in the room, but much of the time they remained untouched. Instead, he devoted significant time to his homework, read magazines, or sat and looked out of his bedroom window. The Hawkins's wanted to honor his self-imposed periods of isolation, but did not want him to feel abandoned or ignored by them.

When I referenced the fights in question, Mrs. Hawkins stated that Omar claimed he did not start the fights. He simply felt compelled to defend himself. I inquired about Omar's behavior and verbal account when he returned home from school on these occasions. She recalled that he never appeared upset when he returned home. Omar would calmly recount the events. He never came across as angry with the people whom he had been in a physical altercation with. It appeared to her that once the altercations ended, he moved on. He believed he was doing what he had a right to do as a matter of self-defense. I asked Mrs. Hawkins's opinion about the underlying cause of the fights. She believed the fights had a racial undertone. Omar was black in a predominately white school. He was unwilling to back down from the teenagers in the school. She added that some of the boys in the school did not like Omar talking to the white girls at the school.

Questions

1. Provide a preliminary assessment of Omar based on the information you have to this point. What are your impressions of Omar?

2. Explore the literature on the adjustment of refugee children in the United States. What are some of the major obstacles to their adjustment?

Foster Parent Background

I asked Mrs. Hawkins for some background on her family. She offered that she was a 52-year-old Caucasian homemaker. She had been married to her husband for 30 years. He was a 52-year-old Caucasian man who worked as an executive for an insurance company. They had two sons, ages 25 and 23, who were both college graduates. The 25-year-old worked in stock investments, and the 23-year-old was in insurance. Neither son currently resided in their home. The Hawkins's lived in a predominately Caucasian community. There were two families from South Korea and one family from India living in the community.

The Hawkins's became foster parents when their older son turned 10 years old. They have had 25 foster children in their home in the past 15 years. Mrs. Hawkins stated that they chose foster parenting because they wanted to give back to society for the blessings that they had received. They believed that they could be good parents to children in need of a home. I thanked Mrs. Hawkins for her time and assistance. I did not conduct a full assessment of the foster home. My intent was to gather a brief background on the environment that Omar was living in. After walking her to the conference room to talk with the foster care worker, I met Omar for the first time.

Meeting Omar

I went to the conference room where Omar and the foster care worker were talking and asked Omar to come back to my office. We sat in the corner of my office occupied by a small couch and two chairs. Omar was over six feet tall and appeared to weigh no more than 160 pounds. His physical appearance was nonthreatening. It would not lead you to believe that he would have been successful in fighting three people.

The goal of the first session was to establish a relationship with Omar and to begin to create an environment where he could relax without fear of retribution. I had to remember that a number of people in authority had told Omar what would happen to him if he did not comply with their wishes. In the first session, I dealt with two issues: his adjustment to life in the United States, and his fights at school. It was important that Omar left the first session with an unmistakable understanding of the consequences of another fight. At the same time, it was important to establish a nonthreatening and supportive atmosphere. Omar has not had many positive relationships with adults.

I made every attempt to create a supportive atmosphere. I began by being honest about why he was there. I left him some control over each session by giving him open-ended categories that he could choose to address. I also showed interest in areas of interest to him. The next step was to talk with him about his interaction with classmates. My goal was to help Omar find new alternatives to fighting.

As part of the foster care worker's plan to keep Omar out of jail, he was an involuntary client. However, once here, he could choose not to participate or invest in the session. My main job was to get him invested in therapy.

There was no predetermined number of sessions for Omar. I believe that treatment plans should reflect the fewest number of sessions necessary for a client to meet his/her goals. Most clients should ultimately be able to function independently of their therapist. My goal, then, is to assist clients in finding ways to problem-solve in the future and move toward independence from me.

Questions

1. Consider the limited amount of information you have on Omar's case. What additional information would you need to fully complete your assessment and develop a treatment plan?

2. With this limited information you have obtained about Omar, inventory his strengths. Please consider both his individual strengths and those available to him within his environment.

3. What strategies have you learned that specifically address working with involuntary clients?

Therapeutic Theory

When working with a client, always keep at the forefront that the client should be the one benefiting from the sessions. The intervention must meet the client's needs and not those of the therapist. An intervention model should emphasize the client's skills, abilities, and understanding of the process. The therapist should continually ask himself/herself, "Is my approach to therapy the best approach for this client?" If the answer is no, the therapist should alter his or her approach. If the therapist is unable to provide the best treatment approach for the client, he or she could refer that client to someone who can best meet the client's needs.

While the treatment plan must be client-centered, I believe that the therapist's comfort is also important. When a therapist is uncomfortable with a particular mode of treatment, the client will respond adversely to that discomfort. The therapist must develop the skills necessary to assist clients in addressing the issues that made them seek help.

My initial approach to therapy incorporates a multi-systemic approach (Derezotes, 2000; Kirst-Ashman & Hull, 1993). This means that as part of the ongoing assessment, I am interested in what the client identifies as the presenting problem, the underlying problem, and any other issues that impact on his or her life. The assessment must include individual and family functioning, social history, group, community, and organizational issues that could have an impact on the client's daily functioning. I want to understand the whole of a person's life. If a therapist only looks at one aspect of an individual's life, or only knows how to work with one aspect of their life, the intervention will reflect that limited understanding.

I bring a foundation of beliefs into every session. I believe in the ability of people to identify issues that are affecting their lives. I believe that family, history, and spirituality affect an individual's beliefs, practices, interaction with, and understanding of the world around them. I also believe in resiliency. Clients often come to us having endured physical and emotional trauma; yet, they continue to survive. That desire to survive is key to any intervention approach.

The other function of a multi-systemic approach is to develop a plan that best meets the client's needs. Is a Person-in-Environment, systems, or behavioral perspective most appropriate for clients? Which perspective best assists clients in addressing the issues that brought them to therapy? Can you use the approach that best meets the client's needs? If you only know how to run groups, will all clients receive group work? These important questions are part of your theoretical framework before working with clients.

My approach is to gather as much information as possible before and during the sessions. I want information on the presenting and underlying problems, if any, and any historical information on the client. If there are any reports, and the release of information forms have been signed, I want to review that information.

Questions

1. Omar is an adolescent refugee from Central Africa. He is living in a Caucasian foster family in a predominantly Caucasian neighborhood. He has been involved in numerous physical altercations at school, and is currently serving a five-day suspension. Given Omar's experience with abuse, isolation, abandonment, grief, and discrimination, what intervention model would you choose to address his multiple concerns?

2. Document how that model addresses race, culture, gender, and religion of refugee children.

Identified Areas

After conducting the initial assessment, I identified three areas that needed further exploration and discussion. The first area was the fighting in school. The second area was the separation and loss he had been experiencing. The third was the abuse and neglect he had suffered. I needed to prioritize those three areas. The issue of fighting was the first area I wanted to address. The rationale behind that decision was the need to keep Omar out of jail. Without addressing the fighting, Omar would not have been available as a client to participate in the other two areas.

Therapeutic Model

Therefore, I decided on a cognitive-behavioral approach to work with Omar. As part of the assessment, it was imperative that I viewed Omar from a micro, mezzo, and macro perspective. I wanted to know what factors affected Omar, and which of those factors Omar had control over. A cognitive-behavioral approach looks at how people think, defines the problems facing them, and determines which problem-solving skills they will employ. Sometimes people simply do not understand why a problem exists, or know how to solve the problem. They may lack an understanding of the true nature of the problem, and they might use misguided problem-solving approaches.

The goal of the cognitive-behavioral approach is to assist clients struggling with negative, irrational perceptions of self by promoting positive change in how they see themselves and their world. Faulty perceptions can make it difficult, if not impossible for some people to engage in healthy relationships or to find appropriate ways to manage difficult situations.

This approach gathers information from early childhood to the present. The client's historical environment can have an impact on how clients function in their adult life. If they carry with them irrational beliefs that cause negative interactions and ways of problem solving, they will react negatively to a normal part of daily functioning. If left unchecked, this negative thought process could lead to such things as sadness, depression, destructive relationships, isolation, and dysfunctional behavior.

Cognitive-behavioral therapy enables clients to change the negative thinking while simultaneously developing positive ways to problem-solve (Payne, 1997). This approach also allows clients to practice new ways of problem solving, thereby empowering them to think differently about future problems that will arise. It is a reality-based way of thinking in determining what control clients have, or do not have, in their daily lives.

However, this approach does not mean that life improves because clients have addressed the negative thoughts that caused faulty thinking. Negative issues from the environment such as discrimination, spousal abuse, and poverty do exist. Those things will not dissipate with the use of cognitive-behavioral therapy. But, the approach may help the clients problem-solve ways to advocate for their needs. Confronting issues both within and outside of the clients' control from a variety of systems is most successful through the multi-systems approach. Cognitive-behavior therapy is not an effective approach for addressing macro issues. Therefore, the therapist must be proficient in a number of approaches, have excellent assessment skills, and possess the inner strength to refer clients to colleagues when they do not possess the skills necessary to effectively work with a client.

Questions

1. The author used a cognitive-behavioral model for working with Omar. Review the literature and outline the basic goals of that approach.

2. The author noted that cognitive-behavioral therapy cannot address the real issues of discrimination, spousal abuse, and poverty. From your review of the literature, expand on the author's assumption that the therapy would not address those issues. Discuss whether you agree with the author. Were you able to find literature that addressed those areas from a cognitive-behavioral approach?

Omar's Life Journey

Omar was born in Central Africa. His mother died shortly after his birth from medical complications. He believed that his father was living somewhere in Africa. Omar did not know whether his uncle was still in the United States or whether he returned to Africa. He was unaware of any relatives living in the United States, and had no contact with relatives in any other part of the world since coming to the United States.

Omar's young life was full of memories of his father leaving him with family members or strangers for months, occasionally over a year, at a time. He expressed feelings of abandonment by his father when he lived with strangers. At times, those strangers cared for his well-being. Other times they treated him like a servant. He remembered being beaten, going days with little food, and working long hours without rest. The beatings included boards across the back, kicks in the stomach, and punches in the face. His father would eventually return for him for short periods, but would eventually leave Omar with strangers again. At times he lived with relatives who he had not known previously. Once retrieved by his father, Omar never had contact with those relatives again.

I asked Omar if the strangers or the relatives treated him better. He took some time to think about it. Finally, he said that the worst treatment came from the strangers, but that more of the relatives were abusive toward him.

Omar did not appear to have any problems talking to me about his life and his family. He maintained eye contact. There was little inflection in his tone. As he described the events of his life, he presented them in a matter-of-fact manner. His body language did not change, nor did he appear uncomfortable as he talked about the abuse, his father's abandonment, the people he lived with, or his uncle leaving him in the United States.

Omar and I developed a genogram in order to see a picture of his family. A genogram is an effective tool in providing a visual of familial constellations and their dynamics. It is a fluid, effective method of treatment revisited throughout the sessions. In constructing the genogram, Omar stated that his father had a number of siblings because he had lived with some of them. He also knew that his father had been married a couple of times before marrying his mother. Those marriages had produced half-siblings who were all older than he was. He had lived with a couple of them when his father took him to England and France.

Omar described his father as verbally and physically abusive to him. He recalls his father using his hands, feet, pieces of wood, or anything else available to beat him. Omar spoke of his father's impatience. He recalled him being quick to yell and threaten those who did not respond in accordance to his wishes. Omar did not understand what the people were supposed to have done, but recognized that they never yelled back at his father.

Living in Different Countries

Moving around with his father, Omar lived in parts of Africa, England, and France. Omar said he never knew why his father moved all the time or where his father went when he left him in the care of other people. He would see papers and airline stubs and noticed that his father traveled to countries other than the ones Omar had lived in. When he was sixteen, Omar and his father met Omar's uncle in England. The uncle was going to the United States and agreed to take Omar with him. Omar remembers pleading with his father not to leave again. Omar expresses the pain of what he thought would be the final separation from his father, because his father had never traveled to the United States. His uncle portrayed the United States as a land of opportunity, telling him if he were going to make something of himself, that was the place to do it.

Coming to America

When Omar and his uncle arrived in the United States, they stayed at a motel for one week. Each day they would go to breakfast and dinner together. After breakfast, the uncle would leave and catch a cab to an undisclosed destination. During the day, Omar would sit around the motel, watch television, or go for walks. Each evening, his uncle would return, claiming to have had a productive day.

Omar recalled his uncle talking about opportunities, chances to make money, and starting a new life. His uncle was always happy and cheerful. He was never abusive, and Omar reported having a good time talking and laughing with him. One day after breakfast, Omar went back to the room and the uncle caught a cab as he did every morning. Back at the room, Omar saw a letter on the bed from his uncle. The letter explained that it was time for the uncle to leave. There were many opportunities in this country and it was time for him to go find them. He had enjoyed the time they spent together, but now it was time for Omar to be a man. The letter told Omar he had the motel for two more days, then to place the room key on the bed and leave. After only one week in the United States, his uncle had abandoned him, forcing him to live in the streets. As Omar talked about the letter, he had the same flat tone and demeanor he did when he talked about the other events in his life.

Omar did not talk about his mother. I wondered if any of the people he lived with ever talked about her. If Omar did not mention his mother, I planned to broach the subject. I wanted to see how she fit in to his life history. As he talked about his experiences, I became aware that he was not ready to discuss her.

A Foreign Land

After leaving the motel, Omar lived on the streets. The weather was warm, so it was easy to find places to stay. He lived in parks and abandoned buildings. After a few months living on the streets, stopping at homeless shelters, and asking for money, he was arrested. The police had noticed him hanging around an abandoned building. Omar had no identification and was taken to jail until he was determined a minor, and not a United States citizen. The police referred Omar to the INS, and he was subsequently placed in a juvenile detention facility. Unable to find any relatives, the INS then placed him with an agency that provided foster care services. The INS classified Omar as an unaccompanied minor and gave him temporary refugee status.

Questions

1. A genogram can be an effective engagement and assessment tool. What components does Omar's case present that would make this a particularly effective tool? Consider both his cultural and historical background when addressing this question.

2. When a therapist first takes inventory at the time of assessment, it is important to recognize this client as a functioning member of multiple systems. Consider for a moment the number of systems at the micro, mezzo, and macro level having an impact on Omar's environment. How can those systems be utilized to benefit the client? What part does the therapist play? The client? Other professionals involved in Omar's case?

3. Considering the immediacy of the presenting problem (the threat of incarceration resulting from the next act of physical violence), what are the benefits of understanding how Omar organizes his life before addressing the issue of fighting?

4. Review the literature on child trauma. How could feelings of abandonment and loss be affecting Omar's functioning? How would that affect his interaction with adults and peers?

School

The Fight Begins

Omar described what he felt was happening at school. According to Omar, some students tormented him with racial insults. Angry at the name-calling, he would retort with physical violence. The school received multiple complaints from families that Omar was terrorizing their children. They called the police after receiving those complaints. According to the police report, Omar was the instigator. He had repeatedly thrown the first punch. Omar offered his feelings of powerlessness in those instances. He felt that the school and the police had not listened to his portrayal of the events. Omar recalled instances when he was not responsible for the first punch, but the authorities placed no credence in those claims. According to Omar, a number of fights were over girls at school. When one of the girls would talk with him, some of the boys would respond by demanding, "White girls are off limits to you." The incident would result in a physical altercation. According to the foster care worker, the school informed her that he fought up to three boys at one time, and Omar always walked away unscathed. The other boys were not so lucky. That story reinforced for parents the notion that Omar was the instigator while the other boys were his injured victims.

Omar said that in addition to the fights over the girls at school, some of the fights resulted after he told classmates of his place of origin. Omar never told people at school that he was from Africa. He told everyone he was from England. He selected England because he knew enough about this country from the number of visits with his father to maintain the ruse. Talking about his place of origin precipitated a change in Omar. For the first time, I saw a major change in his demeanor. He began to play with his hands and the eye contact that he had previously maintained was absent.

Stereotypes

It was apparent that Omar was ashamed of his homeland. While he lived in the United States, the only pictures he saw of his country dealt with starvation, war, and death. He told his peers he was from England, so he did not feel compelled to justify the conditions in his homeland. Many of these students would laugh and call him a liar.

Omar fell into a particular stereotypical category for those individuals. I will refer to the term *stereotype* as Hamilton and Trolier define it, as "a cognitive structure that contains the perceiver's knowledge, beliefs, and expectancies about the human group" (Dovidio & Gaertner, 1986, p. 133). The literature supports the idea that racism is an issue that influences the way people think and interact with each other. The importance of the family in the learning of prejudice must not be underestimated (Allport, 1958). This process of inclusion and exclusion begins at a very early age within the home and school environment. Sager and Schofield conducted the following research involving school-age children. The process involved showing a number of cartoon-like stick drawings to children along with some information provided by the experimenter. One example involved two children sitting in class, one behind the other. One boy continuously pokes the other boy in the back before finally stopping. The children selected the behavior of the actor doing the poking from a list that included the words playful, friendly, mean, or threatening. The pictures varied only by the race of the persons engaged in the behavior. The findings showed that if the actor was black the behavior was more likely classified as mean or threatening. If the actor was white, the actor received the label of playful and friendly (Dovidio & Gaertner, 1986).

Since coming to the United States, Omar experienced the discriminatory and stereotyping practices of others. He had reason to feel isolated from people unlike himself. He lived with a family that cared for him, but to whom he had a difficult time relating and understanding their customs. He remained fearful that the foster parents would abandon him. He lived in a community that did not welcome him, and he attended a school that interacted with him through stereotypes and through derogatory terminology. Despite all of the above, Omar's attempt to protect himself could have led to his deportation.

Questions

1. Review the literature on the definitions of stereotypes. Develop three or four main categories of stereotypes, and discuss which one comes closes to Omar's experiences.

2. Based on your assessment of the case to this point, how should Omar have handled the fighting in school?

3. Interview a person who was subjected to discriminatory and stereotyping practices. Discuss some of their experiences. Explain how they felt about those experiences, and explain how they successfully overcame those feelings, or if those feelings are still a part of their existence.

Omar fought as a way to defend himself and other people of color. His limited understanding of conflict was to fight. He believed that if you allowed people to step on you, everyone would follow suit. He threw the first punch because he felt he needed to strike out before he was hit. An additional concern was Omar's current reputation. Omar did not have to start the next fight. If a teenager hit him, Omar would fight back. With Omar's history, unless an adult was watching, it would be the teen's word against a known instigator.

Lost and Abandoned

Omar was dealing with historical issues of abuse, abandonment, and rejection. He had not had the opportunity to grieve the loss of family members. Omar felt abandoned by his father and extended family. The rejection involved by his uncle leaving him in a foreign land was a viable concern. Omar had never discussed the loss of his mother. He was aware of having half-siblings, some of whom he had never met. He was dealing with issues of identity, new relationships, and cultural experiences, coupled with the challenges involved in the developmental stage of adolescents. All of those issues were having an impact on Omar's life. The first goal remained keeping Omar out of jail.

I believed that Omar's issues expanded beyond individual concerns. There was a need for advocacy on the macro scale. There were a number of steps available for the foster care worker. I made some recommendations to her, but my primary focus was Omar. He was the client referred to me. She needed to address the larger social issues.

Questions

1. In addition to counseling, what other professionals might be involved in Omar's case? How would you as the therapist engage this system of professionals for the betterment of your client? Discuss whether your role should move beyond being the therapist for Omar.

2. The author has identified a number of therapy issues with Omar. What are some of the macro issues that have affected Omar's life? What role should the foster care worker take to advocate for Omar?

Models of Behavior

Omar handled problems based on the models he observed as a child. Those models included threats, physical violence, and emotional abuse. Therefore, during stressful events, Omar returned to the lessons afforded him in his youth. In addition, he projected that model onto other people of color. He felt that physical force was the most effective way to handle confrontation. I asked Omar how he thought people of color handled discrimination. He spoke of what he referred to as, "the strong people fought for what they believed in." His life lessons told him that strong people fought, and weak people took it. I had to wonder if Omar thought of himself as one of the weak people, in accordance to his childhood experiences. If he characterized himself as one of the weak from his childhood, what precipitated his change, to become one of the "strong people who fought"?

The Intervention Model

As I was gathering information from the assessment, I was also thinking about an intervention strategy. The main priority was to keep Omar from going to jail. I could defend Omar's rights—but, if that prosecutor wanted to put Omar in jail, I could not prevent it from happening. One key piece of information was Omar's belief system. From his travels, he had heard and read about the struggles of people of color. He understood that one must fight for their rights. However, he did not understand how they fought. I thought that if I could use a strength-based perspective to introduce some of those people into our sessions, he would gain a better understanding of what it meant to fight (Berg, 1994). Instead of focusing on the problematic issue, this approach takes the skills the person brings to the therapy sessions and uses them to address their problems more effectively.

I asked Omar about any people in history he perceived as those who fought for their rights. He named a number of people. I took one of the people on his list and we talked about him. Omar shared what history he knew about the person and the means he used to fight for freedom. When he finished, I supported him in his knowledge of the person. I asked Omar if I could tell him a little about what I knew about the person. Omar wanted to know more. That was the second time within the session that he showed some emotion. He focused on me, listening to every word. When I finished, he had a number of questions. I answered all the questions that I could and told him when I did not know the answer. The goal of the interaction was to show Omar alternatives to fighting by highlighting the behaviors of those he thought were important.

One effective technique of cognitive-behavioral therapy is bibliotherapy. I used literature as a means to interact with Omar, and a way for him to interact with the topic. This approach often uses literature, music, art, or any form of media that allows the client to interact and explain. We talked about other historical figures he had studied. He was interested in learning more about them. I took the liberty to fill in some gaps on how those individuals had dealt with oppression and discrimination. As we talked, he slowly began to look at alternatives to fighting.

Finally, I gave him a copy of a book and asked if he would read five pages. The book was a symbol of how people dealt with problems in their lives. If he began reading it, it would tell him about the struggles of people of color. The book was a reminder of the session, a symbol of his strength and courage, and hopefully a reminder not to fight. I also wanted a way to give Omar homework for our next session. Homework was a way to reinforce the session and give him a goal that he could attain.

The next three sessions focused on school and the book he was reading. At the second session, he had read five pages. At the third session he had read thirty pages and by the fourth session, half the book. Omar engaged himself in therapy. At each session, he talked about ways of incorporating the readings and our discussion into his daily life.

With the foundation in place, the focus of the therapy turned to his family of origin. We discussed his feelings of loss, rejection, and separation from his family. Omar talked mostly about the people he had been and places he had lived. Future sessions focused on his father. At the fifth session, Omar mentioned his mother. He noted how others talked about their mothers and the feelings of safety they experienced when their mother was around. He believed that if his mother had lived, his father would have remained present in their lives. I took note of Omar's choice of the word "safe" when talking about mothers. It appeared that Omar saw mothers as the protectors of the family.

Questions

1. The author engaged Omar in a discussion about historical figures. The approach appeared effective because the author knew about the people Omar

talked about. Discuss how you would have handled the session if Omar had discussed figures you knew little about.

2. The author used a form of bibliotherapy to connect with Omar. Research the different forms of bibliotherapy. What methods appear to be the most successful? From the literature, give an example of bibliotherapy in use.

3. From the knowledge you have gained, explain if bibliotherapy was an effective tool to use with Omar.

A Surprise

During the fifth session, Omar reached into his pocket and pulled out a picture. He handed it to me and said it was a picture of his mother. I sat there quietly looking at the picture. After a few moments, I handed it back and remarked that she was a very beautiful lady. He looked at me and smiled. When his smile faded, I knew there was something else he wanted to say.

He said, "I don't know if this is really my mother. I think it is, but I am not sure." I inquired about what he meant. Omar said that the woman in the picture was the only picture of a woman around the house, so he took it. He asked his father a couple of times if that was his mother. Initially, his father denied it. The second time he asked his father about the picture, his father slapped him across the face and yelled, "Don't ask me again!" Omar never asked his father again about the picture. His father's emotional reaction led Omar to believe that the person in the picture was in fact his mother.

When placed in the care of different people, he was afraid to ask most of them the identity of the woman in the photograph. He feared the same reaction he received from his father. Omar feared that someone would take the picture and destroy it. He did ask a few people, but they were unsure of her identity. Omar kept the picture safe. Though he remained unsure, he was hopeful that she was his mother.

During the sessions, I wanted Omar to feel comfortable talking about his mother. By showing me the picture, I thought that he was looking for a way to include me in his life. In addition, I assessed that Omar felt comfortable talking to me about her. One of the keys to working with a client is engagement. By providing a safe environment for Omar, it allowed him to discuss his mother without fear of reprisal.

Questions

With the death of Omar's mother, and abandonment by his father, I want you to research the role of parents in a child's life. There is a debate regarding whether parents or peers have more influence over decisions that children make. With younger children, there is limited exposure to outside influences.

However, between the ages of 12 to 18, as children have regular interactions with peers, who has more influence over the child becomes more significant.

1. Research the literature on who has the greater influence over children.

2. What role does the death of a parent have on the development of a child? Review the literature on child development.

3. Omar grew up with the death of his mother and the separations from his father. How would those factors influence his development?

We ended each session with a goal for the next week. I gave him constant praise regarding his ability to stay out of fights. Six weeks into the therapy, Omar had not gotten into another fight. Each session Omar would talk about an incident at school and how he was able to walk away. Omar saw that the people he admired had to control their own lives. They chose how to respond and maintained a calmness that gave them power. Omar still got mad at his peers, but he decided not to let them control his life.

Seven weeks into my sessions with Omar, I received a call from the foster care worker. The INS had found a paternal sister of Omar's living in Florida. Omar had talked to her twice by phone. Omar was coming in that day for his session. The foster care worker told me that would be his last meeting with me. INS had purchased a plane ticket for Omar. He was leaving for Florida the following day to live with his sister.

We talked about his leaving and his thoughts about living with his sister. Omar tried to appear happy at the prospect of seeing his sister. As the session continued, he talked about how much he liked living with the foster family. It was the first time he felt safe. He believed this family would not abandon him. He said he had thought that he would be staying with the foster family and go to college. He also talked about ending the therapy. He expressed his desire to continue. I closed the final session by reviewing the progress he had made.

The case had to close before Omar had a chance to complete the therapy. The treatment plan had been broken into short-term and long-term goals. The short-term goal was to help Omar find alternatives to fighting to stay out of jail. He was conscious and fearful of the inevitability of incarceration in the United States if he was involved in any more fights.

The long-term goals were to move beyond survival; to enhance impulse control, judgment, and coping skills; to develop interpersonal relationships; and to develop some long-term plans for living in the United States. Although progress was made, Omar would have benefited from the opportunity to complete the therapy. Although Omar wanted to see his father, he remained concerned about the possible abuse at his father's hand if he returned to Africa. The foster care agency made a referral to an agency in Florida for Omar to continue in therapy. I am unaware whether he or his sister followed through.

Question

Relationship building is an essential component to effective therapy. Outline some of the tools this therapist used to build a relationship with his client. Can you think of alternative means available to build a therapeutic relationship with your clients? What special considerations are necessary for young clients, or those of a different cultural background?

Evaluation

The therapy with Omar ended when he joined his sister in Florida. When providing therapy with individuals, couples, and families, it can be difficult to evaluate individual cases. With individual cases, the goal is not to generalize the results, but to evaluate the effectiveness of the treatment. Therefore, the task was to evaluate if Omar met the goals of the treatment plan.

Three goals were developed for Omar. The first goal was to help him find alternatives to fighting. The second goal was assisting him with his feelings of separation and loss. The third goal was to address the abuse and neglect he had suffered.

The threat of Omar facing arrest if he got into another fight made this the first area to address. Omar had gotten into a number of fights before beginning therapy. While in therapy, Omar was not involved in another fight. By understanding how people he respected addressed difficult situations, Omar was able to see alternative ways to handle the discrimination he faced at school.

The second and third goals addressed separation and loss along with the abuse and neglect he had experienced. Since the therapy ended before completion, Omar still had work to do in those two areas. He showed progress in his willingness to talk with me about those experiences. In addition, Omar showed me the picture of his mother, demonstrating trust in an adult in a position of power.

Although the therapy was not completed, Omar did make progress. I believed it would be beneficial for him to continue in therapy. At the close of the case, I wrote a report including my assessment, intervention plan, progress, and recommendations. I had no further contact with Omar once he moved to Florida.

Questions

1. As Omar's therapist, you are expected to provide a full assessment to the referring agency for his continued care. Include in this exercise a multi-axial DSM-IV-TR diagnosis, and a summation of your treatment. Do not limit yourself to one presentation per axis. If there were more than one diagnosis, would you prioritize one as primary? Why or why not?

2. Is the DSM-IV-TR an appropriate tool for children born outside of the United States? Explain your answer.

3. **This therapist came to this case with a background working with older children placed in the foster care system, and refugee children from ten separate regions. Without the luxury of experience working with refugee children, would you have taken the case or made a referral? How does the literature and your Code of Ethics align with your decision?**

Bibliography

Allport, G. W. (1958). *The Nature of prejudice.* New York: Doubleday Anchor Books.

Berg, I. K. (1994). *Family-based services: A solution-focused approach.* New York: W. W. Norton & Company.

Berger, P. L., & Luckmann, T. (1972). *The social construction of reality.* Garden City, NY: Doubleday.

Bolea, P. S., Grant, Jr., G., Burgess, M., & Plasa, O. (2003). Trauma of children of the Sudan: A constructivist exploration. *Child Welfare, 82*(2). 219–234.

Derezotes, D. S. (2000). *Advanced generalist social work practice.* Thousand Oaks, CA: Sage.

Dovidio, J. F., & Gaertner, S. L. (eds.) (1986). *Prejudice, discrimination and racism.* Orlando, FL: Academic Press.

Feagin, J. R., & Feagin, C. B. (1999). *Racial and ethnic relations* (6th ed.). Upper Saddle River, NJ: Prentice Hall.

Kirst-Ashman, K. K., & Hull, Jr., G. H. (1993). *Understanding generalist practice.* Chicago: Nelson-Hall.

4

The Leon Family

Dianne Green-Smith

Introduction

This foster care case consisted of William and Marie Leon and their four children. The Leons came to the attention of the child welfare system when their five-year-old son James was found walking down the street at 1:00 a.m. Mrs. Leon had gone out with some girlfriends, and Mr. Leon was parenting the children that evening. Earlier that evening he started drinking alcohol and fell asleep on the sofa. Two of the older children were in their room playing before falling asleep on the floor, and the oldest child, Robert, was spending the night at his cousin's house.

It appeared that once everyone fell asleep, James, who had been sleeping, woke up, looked for someone to play with, and went outside. A few blocks away, a women looking out of her window saw James walking down the street and took him back to her house. Although she knew the parents, she called the police. Later, I found out that she and the Leons did not like each other and have had verbal altercations in the past. When the police arrived, she gave them the address of the Leons' home, and the police and James headed back to the house. After they knocked on the door for several minutes, Mr. Leon came to the door.

Mr. Leon apologized to the police and promised the lack of supervision would not happen again. However, before going to the Leon home, they had called in the address to see if the police had been out to the house before that night. They found out that over the last four years the police responded to the house for domestic violence and fighting with neighbors. With that additional information, they called for Children's Protective Services (CPS) to come to the house and assess the environment.

When CPS arrived at the Leon home, it was not their first encounter with the family. CPS was involved with the Leons regarding issues of intoxication by Mr. Leon. They had also dealt with the children's school truancy, coming to school unclean, and sleeping in class because they would stay up late on school nights. The incident with James, in addition to the previous concerns, and the fact that they did not know where Mrs. Leon was, led the CPS worker to remove the children from the home and file a petition for a preliminary hearing before a judge in the juvenile court. CPS placed the three younger children in an emergency placement foster home. The CPS worker left Robert in the home of his cousin.

Emergency placements are licensed foster families that will take children into their home on a temporary basis until a plan is developed for the children. These are usually well-trained foster parents with experience working with a variety of behaviors. The placements are short term until long-term foster homes that best meet the children's needs are found. When children are placed in a foster care home more equipped for long term care, it frees the emergency foster home for its next placement.

The Court Hearing

The next day was the family's preliminary court hearing. Present at the hearing were Mr. and Mrs. Leon, the CPS worker, an attorney to represent the children, and the judge. The judge asked the parents why James was unsupervised. Mrs. Leon talked about taking a break from being a mother and spending time out with her girlfriends. She said it was seldom that she went out with friends. Mr. Leon said that James leaving the home in the middle of the night was a onetime thing, and it would not happen again. When the judge reminded him that this was not the first time the police and CPS had been to the house, Mr. Leon started talking about all of the problems in his life. He had many medical appointments, and he was feeling depressed last night thinking about the fact that he has AIDS. The CPS worker and the Judge looked at each other, surprised by the revelation. The CPS worker immediately thought about the children's foster family home placement and potential risk factors. The worker looked at Mr. Leon and asked, "Do your children have AIDS?"

Questions

When people hear that someone is HIV/AIDS positive, there are a multitude of reactions. Service professionals are not immune from nervous, anxious, and apprehensive feelings. Working with people engaged in behaviors you disagree with or find repugnant can be difficult to handle. We want you to explore your feelings and reactions when you are confronted by uncomfortable professional situations.

1. Discuss your initial feeling when you found out Mr. Leon has AIDS and the children might have AIDS.

2. Have you worked with someone with AIDS? How comfortable were you, and how did you handle any discomfort?

3. Could you work with AIDS clients? Discuss your answer.

4. Clients have a right to confidentiality. The question is when can that confidentiality be broken. Is there a greater good by breaking the confidentiality? In this case, Mr. Leon has AIDS. It is also possible that the children are HIV positive or have full-blown AIDS. If the children have AIDS, do you tell the foster parents? To fully answer that question, you need to answer some other questions first.

5. What are the federal regulations regarding disclosing that someone has AIDS?

6. What does your state mental health codes say about disclosing that a client has AIDS?

7. If the children are HIV-positive or have full-blown AIDS, do you tell the foster parents? Explain and support your answer.

8. If the children are not HIV/AIDS positive, but a biological parent has AIDS, do you tell the foster parents? What legal or policy mandates would you use to support your decision?

HIV/AIDS Defined

HIV/AIDS is an acronym for Human Immunodeficiency Virus and Acquired Immune Deficiency Syndrome. HIV is a retrovirus that weakens the immune system, thereby decreasing its ability to fight off infections. AIDS is associated with numerous other infections (opportunistic) or secondary infections caused by various bacteria (i.e., protozoa, fungi, etc.). An AIDS diagnosis is given "once an individual has a CD4 or T4 lymphocyte count of less than 200.ul of blood and also tests positive for antibodies to HIV" (Stine, 2001, p. 11).

The Court Hearing Continues

Mr. Leon said that the children were not HIV-positive; therefore, they did not have AIDS. Mr. Leon also took this time to volunteer information regarding Mrs. Leon, saying she was HIV-positive. Mrs. Leon appeared sad at that point and talked about the enormous burden that illness has placed on her family. She talked about their medical appointments and Mr. Leon's medical regime. She admitted dealing with the illness they both possessed was a struggle, that they got depressed at times, and that they did not always handle depression in the most appropriate ways.

Question

Is it a child protection issue to leave the children in a home with one parent that is HIV-positive and the other parent with full-blown AIDS? How does the professional literature define child protection in your answer?

After much discussion, the CPS worker recommended that all four children go under the custody of the juvenile court until a formal hearing decided whether the children should be made temporary wards of the court. She also recommended that the children could return to the biological home if Mr. and Mrs. Leon agreed to work with the foster care agency before the formal court hearing. The CPS worker asked the judge to place in the court order that I should be the worker on the case because of my work within the agency on HIV/AIDS. The family agreed, the CPS worker referred the case, and I was assigned the case. The judge could not order which agency took the case, but if a judge asked an agency director to take a case, that director would comply with the request.

The Referral

After the court hearing, the CPS worker called me regarding the referral. I got as much information as I could over the phone about the family and the court hearing. Another two weeks would pass before I would receive the official CPS report, so any preliminary information was helpful when first opening a case. The Leons did not have a phone, so my only option was to stop by their house. The CPS worker told them that I might come by the house that day, and they were both home waiting for me to arrive.

The Leons lived in an apartment complex in an urban setting. The inside of the apartment appeared clean but lived in. We sat in the living room and talked about the court hearing, my involvement with them, and what we needed to do before the next court hearing. The most important topic was returning of the children to their home, and so we discussed that issue first. Before returning the children home, it was necessary to determine if the Leons had the resources to provide for their physical and emotional needs. Together we explored their resources and their level of preparedness. With everything appearing to be in place, I told them that after our meeting I would pick up their children and bring them back to the house. That also included Robert, who was still living at the home of his paternal aunt. Mr. and Mrs. Leon both seemed a little surprised and relieved that the children were coming home. They thought I was going to say that the children would stay in foster care until I got a chance to know the family. From their original tone, it was clear that they did not have much faith in child welfare services. Because I was bringing the children home that day, the relationship with Mr. and Mrs. Leon began with a level of trust that allowed me entry into their lives. They respected the fact that I was truthful after I kept my word in that instance and in other matters related to them and their children.

Purpose of Referral

The first requirement of any foster care referral is the safety, health, and welfare of the children. The Federal Child Protection Act makes it clear that our job is the protection of children. The relationships we develop with the parents or primary care-takers are important, but they are secondary to the children we are responsible for. The difficulty was trying to develop relationships with clients, which some-times included letting them know that you would not keep certain information confidential.

In the Leon case, the court decided to provide foster care services in the bio-logical home. My job was to assess the family, develop a treatment plan, and work with the family to achieve those goals. This way the children would be safe, and the family would be able to function without further court involvement. To accom-plish that task I met with the family together, and then with the parents and chil-dren separately. I met with the children without the parents in order to establish a relationship with them. I wanted to be certain that there was no abuse or neglect occurring in the home, and that the situation that brought the children to the atten-tion of the child welfare system was not continuing. Children may be fearful of talking about family issues in front of their parents. By meeting with them alone, I try to create an environment in which they can feel free to talk without fear of retribution.

Questions

1. **What is your definition of an involuntary client? How does the literature define involuntary clients?**

2. **How would you approach working with involuntary clients?**

3. **What training or education have you received that specifically prepares you to work with involuntary clients?**

4. **The author was in a dual relationship with the Leons. Because of the court order, there were certain things the author had to address with the family. In addition, the family had areas that they wanted to discuss that only indirectly addressed the court order. After reviewing the Code of Ethics, discuss if the Leons have a right to self-determination if there is a court order.**

5. **What are some of the challenges of a dual relationship? What does the lit-erature say about how a worker can be effective in a dual relationship?**

6. **Discuss whether your responsibility is to the client or the court. Depending on your choice, how does that decision affect the other system?**

7. **Review the Child Protection law and the professional literature, and deter-mine how social workers can uphold the confidentiality of the client. What are the exceptions to your overall findings about confidentiality?**

The Foster Care Worker

I was a foster care worker at a large child welfare agency. That agency provided fos-ter care, adoption, and counseling services through state and county contracts, insurance, and private pay. In the foster care program, case management and therapy was among the services provided to families. My duties included working with the parents, children, foster parents, extended family, community agencies, attorneys, and the juvenile court system. For most of the cases, the foster care worker provided the therapy to the families. The goal was to try to keep families together. When that was not possible, we provided a safe foster care placement for children and worked with the family toward reunification. If reunification was not feasible, we worked to find a permanent adoptive family for those children. As a foster care worker, I had a caseload of thirty children. We did not count the number of families we worked with, but the number of children from each family. That means I could have one family with thirty children or thirty families with one child each. My caseload consisted of twelve families and thirty children. In addition to my background in foster care, I had a background in working with clients positive for HIV/AIDS. Our agency had seen an increase in the number of families infected and affected by HIV/AIDS coming in for services. That neglected population was denied the services and supports they needed. I believed that poor and working class families with HIV/AIDS were a forgotten part of our community.

Questions

1. **What are the statistics in the United States about the number of people with HIV/AIDS? Look for statistics in areas including race, gender, age, income, and lifestyle. Compare the statistics of your state to the national statistics.**

2. **Review the literature on what services and supports are provided to children of HIV/AIDS parents.**

The First Visit

The first home visit was one of mutual assessment for the family and me. They wanted to know my story and my sensitivity to their situation. From a feminist perspective, I explained the agency's involvement and the services we provide. I self-disclosed with the Leons how I had been personally impacted by the virus that causes AIDS, having lost a family member six months earlier.

"Self disclosure enables the therapist to share some of her relevant personal experiences, express her emotional responses to the survivor's experiences, and personally join the survivor's journey to reconstruct her life" (Lundy, 1993, p. 189). In order to establish an "egalitarian relationship" with the Leons, to move toward equality in power, to break down "artificial and unnecessary barriers" (Brown, 1994, p. 104), self-disclosure can also serve to help the client see the worker as a person no different from themselves when it comes to personal challenges. The differences may be in the availability of resources and the process of problem resolution.

The Leons needed to know that I understood (to some degree) their situation, that I empathized with them, and that I connected with them. The expression of empathy has various forms. In our work with people, empathy requires that we reach inside of ourselves to come to an understanding of the experiences of others. With this understanding and with our own subjective experiences, we have the capacity to connect (Gorman, 1993) and to be of service on a level of genuine concern and compassion. Therefore, my work with the Leons began with each of us assessing the other. Since my personal loss of a family member with that disease was most recent (within a year), I recognized how important it was for me to be aware of any countertransference issues I might bring to the table. My issues could potentially be a roadblock for the couple. Talking my concerns over with my supervisor was a much needed requirement so that I could focus on giving the Leons the support they needed to keep their family together.

At the beginning of the case, in order to help the Leons feel more empowered, I explained all of the possible proceedings to them. With that understanding, I outlined the court procedures, the roles and responsibilities of all the players, and the court's expectations of them. A common theme among clients was that they wanted the child welfare system out of their lives. I informed them that they had the power to make that request come true and I advised them that I would help make that request a reality. As a first step, I needed the Leons to sign release of information forms so I could talk to the children's teachers, school social workers, and medical doctors. With the children back in the home, that was one way I could monitor their safety and well-being. Mr. and Mrs. Leon signed all the release forms.

Therapeutic Model

In the Leon case, I utilized the psychodynamic theory of self psychology, the multigenerational systemic theory of Murray Bowen, and a postmodern feminist framework for assessment, intervention, and practice evaluation. The assessment gave particular attention to issues of age, class, gender, power, race, ethnicity, disability, culture, and spirituality. As I conducted the comprehensive assessment, we discussed each area in some detail.

Assessment

The Leon family represented what has become a norm in the structure of an American family. The Leons were a blended family, consisting of Marie and her son Robert, age 10, from a prior relationship; William, who has two children but brought none into that marriage; and William and Marie's three children: Lisa, age 7; Michael, age 6; and James, age 5.

The Leons were an African American family who viewed themselves as ordinary people struggling with normal everyday pressures of living: inadequate income, inadequate housing, inadequate family support, and questionable health. What was unique about the Leon family, however, was that both Mr. and Mrs. Leon were HIV-positive and that Mr. Leon had full-blown AIDS. Mr. Leon was on medication and was routinely seen at a local AIDS clinic. Mrs. Leon was not on medication, but went to the clinic occasionally to have her blood checked to determine her CD4 (a cell that aids in producing healthy antibodies for the immune system) count and to determine her need for future medication. Thus far, Mrs. Leon was determined to be a "slow progressor" and was healthy. Mr. and Mrs. Leon's families of origin were aware of their HIV status. Mr. Leon indicated that he contracted HIV from unprotected sex he had with women while driving trucks around the country. Mrs. Leon was HIV-positive because of unprotected sex with Mr. Leon. Since the awareness of their HIV status, both Mr. and Mrs. Leon occasionally practiced "safe sex" in their marital relationship.

William

William was a 42-year-old male now on social security disability but previously employed as a long-distance truck driver. He enjoyed the freedom of driving and of being his own boss. By taking the jobs he wanted, William decided when he would travel, where he would drive the cargo, and when he would take time off. William described himself as a calm and organized individual who became angry and enraged when he got upset. William indicated that he had been incarcerated a couple of times for poor choices; however, he saw himself as a changed man. He went from being irresponsible to being responsible, especially in terms of being a provider for his family.

William came from a blended family. His mother had two children (a boy and girl), both born out of wedlock before her marriage to William's father. In that marital relationship, however, William was the oldest of five children (four brothers and one sister). Thus, William was one of seven siblings who grew up in a lower middle class existence in the inner city of a large metropolitan city. William identified his father as being a good provider and his mother as a homemaker seeing to the day-to-day needs of the family.

While William saw his father as a good provider, he retrospectively recognized his father as an alcoholic without labeling his father's behavior as such. According to William, his father would drink almost daily. He would hide bottles in the home so as not to frustrate William's mother, who would become disillusioned by her husband's drinking habits. When talking about his father's drinking, William said, "It was not a problem until my mother made his drinking an issue." When his mother would complain, an argument would ensue, sometimes resulting in physical violence toward his mother. William downplayed the violence against his mother. When he described the instances of abuse, William always implied that his mother would instigate the arguments when she knew what the outcome would be. I took note of William's attitude regarding the violence, and wondered about the relationship between William and Marie. I did know from the CPS worker that there had been some violence in the marriage. As I continued the assessment, I would make some determination regarding the scope and depth of violence in the family. Since I spent some time alone with both William and Marie, I could address the issue of domestic violence with Marie without causing her harm by bringing the subject up in her husband's presence.

Although his father had a drinking problem, William saw him as a strong person in the community and a fun person who engaged in activities (working on cars, playing baseball), particularly with William and his brothers on weekends. William stated that not only did his father play with them, but he also included other children in the neighborhood. Although his father gave leisure time to the boys, he did not spend much time with William's sisters, preferring to leave them to their mother.

William did not talk much about his mother except to say that she was nice, a good homemaker who provided them with daily activities, and she was a Christian who took them to church on Sundays. I was unclear about the interaction between mother and child. From his comments, William cared about his mother, but I was unsure if he respected her. He didn't display that same tone of affirmation when talking about his mother. She was a nurturing person, but she may not have been able to mirror to William what was needed in his development—especially if she was constantly oppressed and beaten. It became apparent that William viewed his father as strong and his mother as weak. As I continued the assessment, I planned to explore those relationships further.

Although his mother took the children to church, his father did not go to church because that was his day to rest. William wanted to stay home with his father, but he said that all the children were required to go to church. When younger, William asked his father once why he did not have to go to church. William remembered his father turning and knocking him to the floor, looking down at him, and saying, "Don't question me when I tell you to do something." William remembered that as a valuable lesson and his philosophy was that "children need to know their place. When an adult tells a child to do something, no explanation is required." He added, "That is why so many children are bad today. These parents are trying to reason with their children. That's why their children are talking back to them and to other adults. Who is the parent, the child? I tell you that in my house my children do what they are told, and that's why they don't get into trouble."

I could tell by his expression and tone that he was proud of the fact that his children were good. William thought the use of corporal punishment kept him and his siblings in line. He further believed that approach to discipline would keep more children in line, and that parents could then go back to being parents, rather than their child's best friend. "I can't be both," he said. "I tell my kids, 'I'm not your best friend. That's why I let you go out and play.'" It appeared in some ways that William idealized his father for playing with them, but at the same time, did not see playing with his children a necessary virtue that would enhance their relationship. William had accepted more of his father's authoritarian attributes instead of his playful side.

William expressed a strong bond with all of his siblings. Each brother is a year apart and his sister was born fourteen years after the last brother. William's mother, 66 years of age, was still living; however, his father died at age 62. According to William, there was a significant age difference between his parents.

William had full-blown AIDS and was on medication. William became aware of his HIV status six years ago when he developed Pneumocystis Carinii, a lung infection that serves as an important clue to identify individuals at risk for AIDS. William took his medication as prescribed, but had a constant, nagging cough where he brought up phlegm and spit excessively into a kitchen trashcan. William was hopeful that a cure was found during his lifetime. William did not want to participate in any clinical trials or take new medicines, stating, "I don't want to upset what is currently working regarding my medication." Although I was just getting to know William, he came across as a proud man wanting to be in charge and in full control of his surroundings and of his life. Yet I heard sadness and fear in his voice when he talked about the medications he was on, alternative approaches to treatment, his wife's medical issues, and their financial struggles.

Questions

1. **Make a preliminary list of Mr. Leon's strengths.**

2. **As a child, Mr. Leon lived in an environment where he saw his father abuse his mother. He also saw his mother acquiesce to the abuse. Explore the professional literature on domestic violence to determine if there is a correlation between witnessing abuse as a child and becoming a perpetrator of abuse in adulthood.**

3. **From your assessment of Mr. Leon to this point, was he engaged in any of the behaviors described in the domestic violence literature?**

4. **From the literature, discuss why some men are abusive toward women. Please do not answer the question by discussing why women stay in abusive relationships.**

Marie

Marie was a 27-year-old African American woman who grew up in a single female-headed home in a large metropolitan city. Marie grew up in a multiple high-rise project consisting of low-income buildings that could house a hundred families or more. Marie has one sibling, a sister Kimberly, three years older. Marie and Kimberly had different fathers whom their mother never married. Marie knew her father but she did not have a close relationship with him.

Marie's childhood was one of many disruptions as her mother, who was now 53 years of age, suffered from a mental illness that necessitated hospitalization for months. Marie recalled the first hospitalization of her mother occurred when she (Marie) was about six years of age. During those hospitalizations, Kimberly lived with her maternal grandmother and Marie lived with her maternal great grandmother. According to Marie, her great grandmother served as a substitute mom. She was nurturing, affirming, and a mirroring transference. She encouraged Marie to be successful and to be conscientious about her life and life goals. Marie, however, did not listen to her great grandmother and later regretted that decision. Her great grandmother died at the age of 76 when Marie was 15 years of age.

Marie said she was not close to her mother and that she defied her mother's expectations when she was growing up. Marie said that she was not very close to her sister, as her sister is too outspoken in a "negative way" and that she "whoops and hollers" all the time. Although Marie said she was not close to her mother, she identified characteristics in her mother that were similar to her. Marie said she and her mother were both soft-spoken and that all of them, including the sister, enjoyed a variety of music. She thought that all three of them were alike when it came to relationships; they were attracted to what they wanted, not what they needed. Marie made that statement in a matter-of-fact way. It was as if she had resigned herself and her family to that fate. The powerlessness to change was evident in her voice and demeanor. At age 27, Marie felt oppressed in her relationship with her husband, burdened with parenting responsibilities, unsuccessful in her academic and career endeavors, and "ruined" as a woman for future intimate relationships. Marie felt trapped and did not know how to begin to make significant changes in her life.

First Child

Marie had her first child, Robert, when she was 17 years of age. Marie maintained a good relationship with the extended family members of her son's father, but she did not have a good relationship with the father, John, who was a substance abuser. John was one year older than Marie, and they lived in the same community. John dropped out of high school and worked odd jobs to make money. They met at a house party in the neighborhood. Marie was impressed by John and surprised that he talked to her at the party. She said that all the girls wanted to go out with him, and he had many girlfriends. They started dating, and she soon found out she was pregnant. John said he would help with the care of the baby, but as a substance abuser, he used his money to buy drugs. After Robert was born, John developed relationships with other women and neglected his relationship with Marie and the baby. His family provided financially for Robert and assisted Marie in meeting many of her needs. Robert spent time with his extended family, stayed overnight, and was included in family activities.

Marie saw herself as rebellious during that time, and she dropped out of school. She spent most of her time with John at his parents' house during the day when they were not around. They would hang out with John's friends or they would go to parties. In hindsight, Marie wished she had stayed in school. She saw John and his friends using drugs and drinking, but because she was in love with him, she thought everything he did was wonderful. Their relationship was important to her, and so she looked past his illicit behavior. Marie did not drink or use drugs, but she found herself hanging around people who did all the time. Once she got pregnant, John spent more time with his friends and Marie found herself alone most of the time. She had given up most of her friends to be with John, and now that he was not around, neither were her friends.

Returning Home

Feeling lost and abandoned, Marie turned back to her mother for help. Her mother welcomed her back into the home and assisted Marie with her pregnancy needs. A few years after the baby was born, Marie obtained her General Educational Development (GED) diploma. She felt good about that accomplishment, but felt unsuccessful at other attempts to further her education beyond that point.

Marie had been unemployed, but recently obtained a night job in a nearby factory. Marie was excited to have her own income and to not have to account for every penny provided by William. Before she worked, Marie had to keep track of the money, and could only buy things approved by William. If she wanted things other than groceries or clothing for the children, he had to approve it in advance.

Unlike William, Marie did not have AIDS; however, she was HIV-positive. Marie learned of her HIV status during William's hospitalization for pneumonia. At the time, she was pregnant with James, who the doctors followed medically for the first eighteen months of his life and who was not HIV-positive. Marie maintained regular appointments at the local AIDS clinic for checkups and blood tests. She maintained a healthy CD4 count, was asymptomatic, and was not in need of medication.

Questions

1. **Make a preliminary list of Mrs. Leon's strengths.**

2. **As a child, Mrs. Leon lived in an environment where she saw her mother in powerless relationships with men. She also saw her mother acquiesce to that environment. Review the professional literature on domestic violence. Discuss if the environment that Mrs. Leon grew up in meets any of the definitions of domestic violence.**

3. **From your assessment of Mrs. Leon to this point, was she engaged in any of the behaviors described in the domestic violence literature? Discuss your findings.**

Marital Relationship

William and Marie met through Marie's sister and her husband when Marie was 17 years of age and a single parent. She found herself attracted to William, an older man who possessed a car and other material goods. Marie was young, impressionable, and pursued by William. Although William did not particularly impress Marie's family members, they did not discourage her relationship with him. She saw William as the big, strong figure that would save her from a terrible existence. Marie felt trapped in an environment that she could not escape from, but William could rescue her and take her away to a new life. Because of the age difference, William also replaced the father figure that was missing from her life.

William, on the other hand, had a history of unstable relationships with women and was married during the time he developed a relationship with Marie. Although William did not have children by either of his wives, he was the father of two sons by two other women. William's sons were born when William was

17 and 20 years of age. William talked little about his sons except to say that the youngest one looked just like him. I asked William how much contact he had with his sons. William said, "They are busy so we don't have a lot of contact."

Marie became pregnant early in that relationship and subsequently she and William started living together. In that same year, Marie gave birth to a daughter, Lisa. William separated from his wife and by the end of their second year together, Marie and William had their second child together, a son Michael. A year later, William and Marie had their last child, James. Two years after the birth of their last child, William divorced his wife and married Marie.

During their years together, William worked as a long-distance truck driver until his health prohibited him from driving. Marie also had "small jobs" to assist with expenses around the house. William's social security benefits supported the family. They also received food stamps, Medicaid, and a small child support check from Robert's father. Marie had begun to work and together they were making plans as to how best to integrate Marie's income into the family's budget.

William and Marie moved to their small western community several years ago. Both indicated they wanted to have a different environment for their children, different from the one they experienced. They wanted their children to have the opportunity to play outdoors without fear and threat of danger. Both also desired to live apart from the heavy day-to-day involvement of their families. Although they believed their families could be helpful and supportive when "push came to shove," they saw their families as being intrusive and not as helpful—especially when they needed them during times of great financial struggles. William believed that Marie's family was the least supportive, "rejoicing at her failures instead of rejoicing at her successes."

Although the Leons lived a distance from their families (about three hours by car), they were not isolated. The Leon family was active in a nearby church. The children sang in the choir and Marie worked/volunteered with many of the auxiliaries within the church. Marie said she enjoyed working in the church, as it provided her with an opportunity to "get out of the house." Both also had a network of friends and were able to engage them in pleasurable activities. Concerns expressed by each of them regarding those activities centers on the amount of money spent by Marie and the amount of drinking William indulged in.

Questions

1. Assessment is an ongoing process. What are some of your initial impressions of the Leon family?

2. What HIV/AIDS related resources are in your community? How are those resources accessed? Where does the funding come from to provide those services? Is there adequate funding to meet the funds of that population?

Problems Identified

Both Marie and William had been engaged in individual and conjoint therapy with me in their home. We met twice a week, in the late afternoon, while the children were in school. I wanted a time to meet with the parents without the distraction of the children running around. That time allowed the parents to talk freely, and to not involve the children in adult conversations. I also met with them in the late afternoon because after our session ended, I could meet with the children arriving home from school. There had been six home sessions over a three-week period. There were still four weeks before the formal court hearing. Both William and Marie were engaged in the therapeutic process. Together, they had identified problems related to communication between the two of them, inadequate finances, inadequate transportation, multigenerational family issues, health issues, trust issues, housing issues, and the court system. Although one could argue that the court hearing was the most important issue, I tried to balance their identified problems against the reason I was involved with the case. I believe clients should take some ownership of the sessions, therefore investing in treatment. In addition, every day that I was in their home, it was a constant reminder of what the presenting problem was. As clients address the problems they have identified, they can then make progress toward the main objectives: ensuring that the children are safe, and getting me out of their lives.

William struggled with the court's involvement with his family. He acknowledged James's lack of supervision, but he felt that it was a mistake that would not happen again. When I asked about CPS and the police coming to the house, he blamed it on neighbors, some of Marie's relatives, and the school. "People act like no one gets upset," he said. "We get mad in our family. My father got mad and my brothers get mad. Sometimes I get mad. I wish people would leave us alone." William stopped talking, looked at Marie and then turned to me. "I'm sorry. There are a lot of things going on, and I just can't handle everything sometimes."

Marie sat quietly while William talked. She would look at him, but I could tell she was also looking for my reaction to William. It appeared she wanted to say something, but decided not to interrupt. I asked Marie if there was anything she wanted to add to the conversation. She wanted to know what they needed to do so they did not have to go back to court.

I told William and Marie that the court hearing was scheduled and they would have to attend. However, the progress they made would help the judge make the decision they desired. I acknowledged that their past relationship with the legal system could be a factor in the judge's decision; that was why they needed to demonstrate progress before returning to court. I reminded them, "The CPS worker saw something positive in you. She could have placed your children in foster care until the formal hearing, but she said the children could go home until that time. She also asked the court to request me as your foster care worker. She could have asked for someone else or not made a request at all. However, she wanted me to work with you because she thought we could work together. She saw something that made her advocate for you."

It was hard for the Leons to accept what I was saying, but they were willing to work with me. They answered my questions, provided personal information, and talked about their relationship. I still felt that there were some things they were not sharing, but everyone likes to keep some of their personal life private. As we continued to talk, I believed they would share more of their life.

Another issue addressed in the sessions was William and Marie's health. They had informed their families of their HIV status, but decided not to tell their children. Although the children knew that William was sick and was taking medicine, they thought the medicine was for chronic bronchitis. William and Marie had no immediate plans to inform the children of their health status, as both expected a long life. They had also made no concrete plans for the care and provision of their children should their health change into a symptomatic stage resulting in other caretaking needs.

Questions

1. The foster care worker is providing therapy in the home instead of the office. What are the strengths and weaknesses of each approach? Review the literature on both approaches.

2. When reviewing social work history, traditional social work was fieldwork. Today, office work is traditional social work and fieldwork is nontraditional. Discuss the reasons why you think this change occurred. Interview professionals engaged in either of the approaches and discuss why they chose that approach. How do they know their approach is in the best interest of the client? Also ask what theory supports their position of traditional and nontraditional social work.

Self Psychology, Systems Theory, and Feminist Theory

Going into a client's home offers me unique challenges. Often times, as with the Leons, a home visitor is not provided with all the basic details regarding the home. The visitor would not know that the family lives upstairs, not downstairs, or that the doorbell works or doesn't work. Sometimes, as with the Leons, there is no telephone to confirm visits. Also, sometimes, as in my case with the Leons, I am not sure who will be in the home, whether or not there is a private meeting area, and exactly who will be involved in the therapeutic process.

The reason I like meeting with clients in their home is so I can see them function in the environment that is most real to them. I see the office as an artificial setting that tells me little about how parents interact when all the pressures of life are closing in on them. In the home, people come to the door, children play and fight, and all of the duties of daily life impacts how people function. This is a true picture of family life. I want to see that interaction and help them mange the stress so they can provide the appropriate care for their children. Many of the clients whose children are in foster care have no transportation. Some of the families use public transportation to get to the agency for visits with their children or to keep counseling appointments. Some professionals would argue that parents who make it to the agency have begun the process of growth and commitment toward their children. I thought it meant that they knew how to catch the bus, but it told me nothing about their ability to parent, protect, or handle the stress of providing for their children. The time they spent on the bus was time we could have made progress toward reunification of their children. So, whenever possible, I work with my families in their home.

Family Roles

I was able to observe the display of roles within the spousal system. While I was in their presence, the Leons appeared to lead a male-dominated lifestyle. In actuality, Mr. Leon took the lead in those activities that were routinely established for women—cooking, cleaning, washing clothes, and maintaining the home in some "respectable order." From a feminist perspective, I was confronted with societal "beliefs and stereotypes about what is normal, natural, and to be expected" (Brown, 1994, p. 99). There was no difficulty in observing Mr. Leon work in a role which was traditionally described as female work, as I also grew up in and lived in an environment where men routinely do work considered feminine by traditional American culture and standards. What was interesting was from the conversations we had, the roles of dominant and submissive within Mr. Leon's family of origin clearly depended on gender. William talked about his father as someone he wanted to be like. The image of his father was one of men doing men's work and women doing women's work.

When the Leons described their work duties around the home, it did not fit the image they first presented. Due to medical issues and the need for money, families adapt to the needs of their environment. In order to provide and keep their family together, William and Marie had to change some of their roles. The traditional husband and wife roles did not fit their circumstances. However, there are physical and psychological traditional roles in a family. While William engaged in more of the domestic roles, and despite his physical limitations, he was still the man of the house. Marie and the children all understood their roles and tried to meet the expectations imposed by William.

The Genogram

While I assumed a feminist stance in my approach to the Leons, I also used a multigenerational systems approach. I was aware of some of the psychodynamic relevance of the couple as individuals. As I worked with the Leons, we discussed their relationship with their children. Mr. Leon took the lead in the discussion and began to address similarities he was aware of in his sons in comparison to characteristics he acknowledged in his brothers. I took that as an opportunity to introduce the genogram concept to the couple, not only to explore similarities and differences, but also to assess with the couple dynamics of family relationships, patterns of functioning, triangles, levels of differentiation, polarization, and other pertinent family patterns (Nichols & Schwartz, 1998). The genogram was both an assessment tool and an intervention technique. It enabled the Leons to view their problems from a multigenerational perspective regarding their childhoods and current experiences in their own household. The genogram would help them redirect any projection and blaming and change their communication patterns.

Questions

1. The foster care worker used the genogram as an assessment tool. Discuss how you would use a genogram as an intervention tool.

2. The Leons and the author talked about traditional and nontraditional families. How would you define traditional and nontraditional families?

3. How would you define your family? Discuss the behaviors in your family that helped you define them as a traditional or nontraditional family.

William: Genogram

I started a rough draft of the genogram with Mr. Leon first as a strategy to gain his trust. Mr. Leon began by describing family members in birth order, giving their names and genders. From that point, we were able to move up to prior generations. He provided information on his maternal grandparents and maternal great-grandparents. Mr. Leon was able to provide information on his paternal family as well.

In discussing the genogram at a later session, Mr. Leon described in more detail his father's role in the family. Mr. Leon valued his father as a man with great technological gifts and great organization skills. Mr. Leon talked earlier of how his father passed his technological skills to his sons. Mr. Leon has already started this process with Michael, the son whom he affectionately called "Fuzz." Mr. Leon also talked about his relationship with his stepson, Robert, and shared how he was just beginning to teach Robert those same skills. According to Mr. Leon, Mrs. Leon prevented him from having a strong role in Robert's life. Therefore, Mr. Leon distanced himself as a father figure, leaving Robert more to his mother just as Mr. Leon's father left Mr. Leon's sisters more to their mother.

Although Mr. Leon talked about dynamics displayed in his family of origin, it remained unclear what role his father played in the lives of Mr. Leon's older half siblings and stepchildren. It is quite possible that his mother felt the need to protect those children from her husband's emotional outbursts or "different treatment" just as Mrs. Leon felt the need to protect Robert from physical discipline used by Mr. Leon. Systemically, one would look at those dynamics as triangulation between

William, Marie, and Robert. Emotional fusion between Marie and Robert also existed, and it played a major role within the sibling relationship as with Mr. Leon and his older half siblings.

Sibling rivalry can become an inevitable outcome of triangulation. Marie's preoccupation with her attempts to protect Robert would not enhance his status with his siblings. Mr. Leon's preoccupation with passing on skills he learned from his father only to his son, Fuzz, will not allow Robert to properly differentiate from his mother and develop healthy relationships with his siblings. According to a study done by Frits Boer and others at the University of Leiden in the Netherlands in 1990:

> Siblings were aware of partiality not only toward their siblings, but also toward themselves; firstborn children reported more positive behavior toward themselves from second born siblings than did second born children with regard to their older siblings; siblings with brothers reported more competition than did siblings with sisters, regardless of their own sex and perception of parental care by the children was highly correlated with the perception of the sibling relationship—a more negatively judged parent-child relationship coincided with a more negatively judged sibling relationship. (Nichols & Schwartz, 1998, p. 147)

There was much to learn from Mr. Leon's genogram. I would continue to use the genogram to assess multigenerational dynamics, to evaluate the impact family of origin had on that family, the level of fusion as well as differentiation, cutoffs and triangulation.

Questions

One of the challenges of a blended family is agreeing to roles and responsibilities. Mr. and Mrs. Leon both agreed that William is not as close to Robert as they would like. However, they have different explanations about the reasons for the distance between the two of them.

1. What are the reasons that Mr. and Mrs. Leon gave for the distance between William and Robert?

2. Stepparent relationships can be strained when people feel they have to choose sides. From a review of the literature, what are some of the difficulties in stepparent relationships?

3. How should those difficulties be addressed?

Marie: Genogram

Mrs. Leon demonstrated eagerness to work on her genogram after sitting through William's genogram. Marie's genogram showed four generations because her family was younger and family members were still living. Marie had to guess at the ages of her maternal and great maternal grandmothers. It was quite possible that those ages were not correct, as the genogram indicated that Marie's grandmother had her first child when she was thirteen years of age. Of course, if that was so, it could indicate a pattern of early child bearing.

While developing Marie's genogram, we outlined patterns of communication within the maternal line, characterizing people as harsh (outspoken) or nice and submissive (soft-spoken). Mrs. Leon became aware of a physical ailment, migraine headaches, as being transported within their family. She saw their love of music as a social outlet. The genogram also provided Marie with an opportunity to share a little about her mother's mental illness, her hospitalizations, and the break up of the family during that time when Marie and her sister lived in different family households, cut off from one another for months at a time. The messages Marie received during those times were unclear, although Marie recalled her mother's hospitalization when she was young and continuing through her adolescence. As she became older, Marie found she had little respect for her mother and challenged her at every opportunity. Marie did not see her family as an emotionally supportive unit, which made it easy for Marie to seek distance by moving away from her family.

Marie began to see patterns in her family of origin. She recognized a similar pattern of relationships in herself, her mother, and her sister. They all had relationships with the same types of men, had children at a young age, and had men who were uninvolved in the raising of the children. Marie began to see her sister in a new perspective. She also felt badly about how she treated her mother. Marie always thought her mother was weak. Now she wondered if she was just trying to survive. If her mother lacked the strength and power to change her life, how could she pass that on to her daughters? Marie was still trying to figure things out, but she had begun the process of self-examination. She knew there were more questions than answers. But, there were answers if she decided to look for them.

Ongoing Assessment

Mr. Leon lived in a home where he had to compete for his mother's attention, never believing that she loved him. Mr. Leon was not able to understand how exhausted or overwhelmed his mother was. However, he perceived closeness with his mother (the primary mirroring selfobject) as having never occurred. Fourteen years after the last male child was born, Mr. Leon's mother gave birth to a daughter. That same year, Mr. Leon had a son himself. He had moved out of the home at age 16, continued in school, obtained a job, maintained an apartment, and became involved in street activities in order to fill deficits resulting from inadequate transference.

Once on his own, Mr. Leon became quite narcissistic and grandiose in his thinking and behavior. He eventually dropped out of school, ran into trouble with the law by stealing and breaking into banks, and landed himself in jail in a southern state for four years. While in jail, he met a woman who was visiting another inmate and married her for "conjugal visits." Mr. Leon saw this woman as a selfobject whom he could attach himself to in order to "merge" with that person for a sense of "protection, warmth, and security"—things missing from childhood.

Mr. Leon had other unfulfilled relationships with women that were empty, as he had very little personally to give to those relationships. Mr. Leon was a frustrated human being with no healthy "internalizations" from his primary selfobjects. After serving time in a southern jail, Mr. Leon returned to his home in the large metropolitan community. His father was deceased by that time and Mr. Leon moved in with his mother. At some point, Mr. Leon, who was living a street life, got into an argument with some people, left the scene, and came back with a gun. Mr. Leon fired the gun several times, killing the individual with whom he argued. Mr. Leon received a twenty-three-year jail sentence, but served ten years for good behavior. Mr. Leon said he did not know who he was as a person when he took the other man's life. He knew there were consequences for his behavior. In terms of his own psychology, Mr. Leon was not yet cohesive. According to Reppen (1985), Mr. Leon's apparent pathology appeared in the overall structure of the self where failure in the selfobject relationship in childhood or adult life leads to painful experience of fragmentation. Mr. Leon said, "Looking back, I did not know who I was, but I knew that I took a life and I knew there were consequences for my behavior. I felt nothing when I shot that fellow. I hid for months until I got tired of running and just gave up. I delivered myself to the police because I was tired of running and hiding."

After serving time in jail, Mr. Leon trained as a long-distance truck driver and was able to obtain a job in that trade. Mr. Leon also became involved with women, had another son, married another woman, and met his present wife, Marie, while he was still legally married. Mr. and Mrs. Leon began cohabitating together in Mr. Leon's house. His wife move out and after three years of legal separation they divorced. Mr. and Mrs. Leon had three children before their marriage. Mr. Leon said he was not able to make a full commitment to Marie. I surmised that Mr. Leon's emptiness and his lack of love from his primary selfobjects prevented him from having fulfilling relationships. For a while, those women served as selfobjects that could sooth and calm Mr. Leon's internal struggles. Those relationships were insufficient to meet his total needs, and so alcohol and other substances triangulated into the marriage.

Unmet Needs

Mrs. Leon's narcissism presented itself differently from Mr. Leon's primarily due to gender, cultural, and socialization issues. Mrs. Leon experienced similar deficits in her childhood because of her mother's mental illness and hospitalizations, and because of Marie's separation (inevitable disruption of the sustaining selfobject relationships) (Kohut & Wolf, 1978) from her sister. While Mrs. Leon saw her mother as not meeting her needs and as an inadequate parental selfobject, Mrs. Leon saw her affectionate maternal great grandmother as her mother's substitute. Idealizing mirroring transferences occurred. The grandmother was empathetic to Mrs. Leon's needs, allowing a healthy internalization to occur. It appeared that the grandmother was perhaps the selfobject that allowed for healthy transmuting internalizations and thus prevented the self of Mrs. Leon from becoming damaged or weakened (Elson, 1986).

As she became older, Mrs. Leon became more grandiose in her thinking. She was more rebellious toward her mother, and greater tension developed between them with Marie's desire to "be grown." When their mother was hospitalized, Marie and her sister were left alone in their apartment to take care of themselves, while family members would check up on them daily. Most of the time there was no "authority" figure in the home, and no mirroring or idealized parental image. There was no father, and the older sister had in effect become abusive toward the mother. The sister physically pushed her and verbally threatened her when she was home. Poverty was another factor for the family. There was the fear of mental illness being an inherited factor that entered into Mrs. Leon's thoughts and increased her low esteem and feelings of unworthiness. Mrs. Leon experienced her mother as being self-absorbed and emotionally detached. There were other times when Mrs. Leon experienced her mother as "somewhat involved." For the most part she experienced her mother as fragile, as an unavailable caretaker, and as a peer or pal. She never characterized her mother as a mirroring selfobject.

The Family Secret

It was not until much later that Mrs. Leon learned from a family member that a step-father sexually abused her mother's sister and physically abused Mrs. Leon's mother. Mrs. Leon says her mother did not acknowledge any sexual abuse. It was possible that the stepfather also sexually abused her mother. The grandmother was unable to provide protection for her daughters or serve as a mirroring selfobject. There again was trauma, pain, and selfobject failure. Mrs. Leon's mother was not able to give her daughters what she herself had not internalized through her relationship with her mother, the failed mirrored selfobject or her relationship with her stepfather, the idealized selfobject. The sexual and physical abuses were traumatizing and prevented cohesion. From a feminist perspective, the maternal grandmother, mother, and daughter all experienced powerlessness in a male-dominated world.

Mrs. Leon grew up without any adequate primary mirroring selfobject. No one served in a daily ongoing caretaking and nurturing role. As a result, there were structural deficits in need of repair. Mrs. Leon also dropped out of school where perhaps she might have been in a position to meet others who could have served as missing selfobjects for her. Instead, Mrs. Leon became sexually active and gave birth to her son when she was 17 years of age. The child's father was involved with drugs and he too was not an idealized parental selfobject for his child.

Mrs. Leon, as stated earlier, eventually met and dated Mr. Leon. Mrs. Leon had emptiness resulting from a physically absent father and an emotionally absent mother. Mr. Leon had a need to be more like an ideal father rather than the type his own father had been. Mr. Leon, in some ways, became a "father" to Mrs. Leon. He provided her with stability and nurturance for a while, and he validated and admired her. But later problems and conflicts occurred as both struggled with parenting issues and narcissistic injuries and deficits. Mr. and Mrs. Leon needed healthy transferences that would help to reduce and eliminate abusive multigenerational patterns.

The Children

I met with the children during every home visit. I saw some of the same stages in them that their parents experienced in their childhood. They were seeking attention from their parents. They were looking for both mirroring and idealizing selfobjects. Lisa, Michael, and James appeared more attached to their parents than Robert was.

Robert was able to verbalize that he was not as close to his stepfather as the other children were with their father. Robert was struggling in school, has difficulty making friends, and had little contact with his biological father. He had contact with his paternal relatives, and he enjoyed those visits. Robert was seeking closeness to his father through his relatives. He would ask if anything belonged to his father and, if the answer was yes, he asked to have that item. He would ask relatives what things his father liked, how he had fun, and whether his father asked about him. Robert got into trouble, hoping that someone would spend time with him as a result. I believe his acting out was a cry for his father to rescue him. Robert's acting out behavior was not out of hand, but there was concern it would get worse if he thought it would bring his father back into his life. Mr. Leon always said that his biological children did not get into trouble. That needed further discussion.

Lisa and Michael also have some attention-seeking behaviors. Although they were living with their biological father, there was still distance in the relationship. Mr. Leon was trying to find his connection, his place. That did not leave room for his children to receive the amount of emotional attention they needed.

The children saw their mother as kind, loving, and weak. She did what their father told her to do. They knew if she told them one thing and their father told them something else, they had to do what their father said or risk getting into trouble. Robert, Lisa, and Michael described their mother the same way Mr. and Mrs. Leon described their mothers: ineffective, weak, and submissive. Robert also viewed his mother as needing protection from Mr. Leon. That could cause potential problems, especially as Robert got older and the relationship between Mr. and Mrs. Leon remained the same.

Questions

1. **What are the data on sons protecting their mothers when they are in abusive relationships?**

2. **Review the literature on why sons would protect their mothers. Explain how they protected their mothers and what the outcomes were of the sons' actions.**

3. **Discuss some steps that could prevent Robert and Mr. Leon from engaging in that type of interaction.**

I talked with the children about the discipline they received from their parents. Their mother yelled at them to stop engaging in the behavior. She had hit them a few times, but not very hard. She would say, "If you don't stop, I'm going to tell your father." They said that their father was the one that hit them when they got into trouble. I asked whether they knew the kinds of things they got into trouble for were wrong. Robert, Lisa, and Michael all said they knew it was wrong, but they did it anyway.

I asked who got into trouble the most, and everyone pointed to Robert. Lisa said that her mother would not tell her father when Robert got into trouble because he got into trouble all the time. Robert agreed that he was punished the most, but he did not feel that he did more things wrong.

Medical Examination

The agency's medical doctor saw all four children. There were no bruises on the children other than the ones that came from normal living. The doctor saw no indication of physical or sexual abuse. In his conversation with the children, they gave him no indication of abuse.

School Personnel

I also talked to the school social worker from each school. None of the social workers saw any indication of child abuse. A couple of the school social workers had called CPS about the children's attendance, lack of attention in class, and inappropriate dress. In individual sessions with school officials, they did not believe that their parents abused the children.

Evaluation

Learning about the dynamics with both Mr. and Mrs. Leon's family of origin had been an ongoing process. Although self psychology helps to understand the family's developmental history and how it influences their current behavior, it was not the most obvious form of treatment in the therapeutic process to that couple. I was hoping to provide the couple with a new kind of experience so that the couple/client within the transference relationship could work toward meeting their own needs. The therapeutic process provided a corrective emotional experience within the environment and explanations help clients see that what they did or what they felt or how they were relating to me made perfect sense given their history. Empathic understanding and subsequent mirroring were essential to the family's therapeutic process.

Systems theory lends itself to feminist practice. It is based upon the concepts of differentiation of the self and anxiety due to emotional fusion. As I addressed the

Leons through that kaleidoscope, I was mindful of the fact that women are relational and view themselves through their relationships with others. These relationships interact from a nondeficit perspective. Marie perceived, at that time, reciprocity in her relationship with her husband. That relationship appeared to have allowed Marie to bond with a male and to work toward greater maturity as she aged. Marie had not yet connected her husband's past job as a long distance driver as similar to her mother's absence from the home due to her hospitalizations.

As part of the assessment, I had reviewed my work with the Leon family from three perspectives. The process was slow and rewarding. There continued to be challenges to doing home visits: children home from school, a small house that did not allow for privacy, and friends dropping in. Being able to pick up from where we left off was not always a smooth process, and almost seldom occurred on consecutive sessions.

During the process of working with that family, I had been aware of my own countertransference and I had addressed it through the process of supervision. Perhaps the concern in working with a couple where the wife became infected due to the careless lifestyle of her husband was cause for some initial anxiety. I discovered that I was not angry with Mr. Leon. In fact, I was able to develop empathy for him just as I had felt empathy for Mrs. Leon. That empathy emerged through the process of getting to know and understand the Leons' individual histories as well as the history of their struggles as a family. Both wanted the best for their children, but they were so influenced by their past, by the expectations of family, and by the larger society that they remained in a cycle of patterns of behavior.

As I continued working with the family, utilizing therapeutic approaches that would provide meaningful interventions for them, I saw that the Leons were ready to make changes in their lives. They just needed help from someone who could accept them as they were, who could be stable and empathic, and who could provide them with a healthy mirroring transference. There was much for them to learn about one another. There was much more they needed to learn about their disease and how it might affect their family. There was much to prepare for in order to live their lives as completely as possible. The Leons' evaluation of me as I worked with them was ongoing. My evaluation of the Leons continued in order to make sure I met their needs.

Questions

Now that you have reviewed the case, you will need to make some decisions about your intervention strategies.

1. **What are the main issues that the Leons wanted to work on?**

2. **What are the issues you have identified that the family needs to address?**

3. **Explain why you think the children should remain in the biological home or be placed in foster care.**

4. With your review of the Leon family, develop the goals for the case.

5. Develop a treatment plan for the Leon family. Include what the family and you will do to achieve those goals, and discuss how you will know when the goals have been achieved.

After reading the case, you should still have one significant question to answer.

6. Why do you think that Marie never expressed any anger toward William for making her HIV-positive?

Bibliography

Brown, L. (1994). The relationship in feminist therapy. In *Subversive dialogues: Theory in feminist theory,* 92–123. New York: Basic Books.

Elson, M. (1986). *Self psychology in clinical social work.* New York: W. W. Norton & Co.

Gorman, J. (1993). Postmodernism and the conduct of inquiry on social work. *Affilia, 8*(3), 247–264.

Kohut, H., & Wolf, E. (1978). The disorders of the self and their treatment. *International Journal of Psychoanalysis, 59,* 413–425.

Lundy, M. (1993). Explicitness: The unspoken mandate of feminist social work. *Affilia, 8*(2).

Nichols, M., & Schwartz, R. (1998). Bowen family systems theory. In *Family therapy concepts and methods,* 141–175. Boston: Allyn and Bacon.

Reppen, J. (1985). *Beyond Freud: Study of modern psychoanalysis theorist.* Hillsdale, NJ: Analytic Press.

Stine, G. (2001). AIDS update 2001. Upper Saddle River, NJ: Prentice Hall.

5

Dan

Brian J. De Vos

Introduction

In foster care there is a concept called "aging out of foster care." This concept refers to children who have lived in the foster care system until their 18th to 21st birthday (depending on the state they lived in), or who have any medical or developmental issues that require continued support and supervision before they are discharged from the children welfare system to live independently as adults. Some of these children leave with the skills to live an independent and successful life. Others leave lacking the ability to maneuver the responsibilities of adulthood. There are stories of eighteen-year-olds lacking the skills to balance a checkbook, find a job, or maintain a residence after spending up to fourteen years in the foster care system. There are independent living programs with the primary goal of preparing these children for adulthood. Some are successful at achieving that goal. However, not all children receive or have the ability to fully implement the services offered. They spend the majority of their life in different types of foster care settings, never developing a true sense of family.

What happens to those children who grow up in the child welfare system once that system is no longer available to meet their daily needs? What important skills are learned in a family, and how do you gain those skills when you don't grow up in a family? Is family stability important in leaning how to function, or can a child move from placement to placement and learn those skills? These experiences are affecting children as they are aging out of the foster care system. The answers could have a profound effect on children in the foster care system, and on those who saw foster care as their only family.

This case looks at a young man who "aged out" of the child welfare system, but is still struggling with some of the issues in adulthood that he was trying to overcome in foster care. His experiences in foster care, biological family interactions,

and struggles with the normal developmental stages of adolescence have all affected his adult functioning. He has been in outpatient mental health counseling, group
services, regular foster care, residential treatment, and therapeutic foster care—all
as a result of family dysfunction, abuse, and neglect. When he seeks help from a
therapist that was part of his childhood, therapeutic treatment and ethical issues will
all converge on their sessions.

    The case study follows the therapeutic relationship and treatment progress of
a client who spent most of his childhood in the child welfare system. The case
begins with a brief history of my involvement with the client and my psychosocial
assessment. I have outlined the journey and struggles with abuse and neglect this
young person experienced in the early years of his life, through the treatment modalities and the treatment plans where one can see the psychosocial and psychological
hurdles this young man was facing. Traveling briefly through the treatment stages
reveals the vast amount of work required for a young person to overcome the ill
effects of severe family dysfunction, abuse and neglect, abandonment, and separation and loss issues. Finally, this case includes information on past therapeutic information and presents an overview of the client's final formal treatment experience.

Searching for a Therapist

I was a therapist at an outpatient mental health agency when I took the case. The
agency worked with self-referred and court-mandated clients. The agency provided
two programs: one-half of the building provided adult services, and the other half of
the building worked with children. I worked on the adult wing providing therapy to
individuals and couples. One year earlier, I had worked in a foster care agency in
their intensive foster care program. It was at that agency that I first met Dan. Dan,
who was seeking counseling, had called the foster care agency looking for me and
was told where I was working.

    I was surprised to see Dan. Five years had passed since my last session with
him. I had to admit that there were times I wondered how he was doing, but I never
thought I would see him again. My job was to work with a client in a therapeutic
relationship, not to have a relationship outside of that setting. When people seek
assistance or are in a vulnerable state, it is inappropriate to have anything other than
a professional relationship. The role of power in a client/therapist relationship is
fraught with the abuse and misuse of the power we have to influence those we
should be helping.

    Due to our previous professional relationship, I wondered if I should see him.
I believed that he had formed more than a therapeutic relationship with me at the
time of our professional involvement because I was one of a few people who accepted him. There are times when clients can misinterpret the relationship. I am aware
of clients who wanted a relationship with their therapist because he/she was the
first person to listen to them and support them. Clients have viewed therapists as
mothers, fathers, best friends, and fictive kin. A counselor listens, gives feedback,
problem-solves, and encourages clients to achieve their goals. Clients can misinter-

pret the skills the counselor brings to the sessions with the forming of a relationship. When a client misinterprets the relationship, transference occurs.

There were times in our previous relationship when Dan wanted to look at me as a big brother or father figure; however, most of the time he saw me as his social worker. I wondered how our past would influence the current therapeutic relationship. At the same time, Dan was seeking help and that was a possible sign of good problem-solving skills. The fact that he asked for me could have demonstrated his ability to form relationships and seek assistance from those who have been positive in his life. Until I met with him, those were only questions without answers.

Questions

1. The author had a prior professional relationship with Dan. Based on the information you have, discuss the reasons why the author should or should not work with Dan. What does the professional literature and Code of Ethics (NASW, 2000) tell you about proceeding with this case?

2. If a client sees the therapist in a nontherapeutic way, should the therapist refer the client to another therapist? Discuss your reasons for the choice you made. What does the literature say about transference and how does that impact on your decision?

My History with Dan

My therapeutic relationship with Dan was not one of my typical cases. I have known him since he was 10 years old. I first met Dan while in my internship, as part of my master's of social work degree requirements, at a residential facility for boys. Dan and I came to the facility at the same time. I worked with Dan on some of the behavioral issues that affected his ability to interact appropriately with peers and adults. Dan's father had sexually abused him and it was having an impact on his daily functioning. Bedwetting, stealing food, and sexually abusing his younger sister were all by-products of his sexual abuse and chaotic home life.

After completing my internship, I left the agency and continued my career in child welfare working at a foster care agency. I met Dan five years later when I returned to the site of my internship to work in their therapeutic foster care program. Since age 12, Dan had been living in a therapeutic foster home. I worked with Dan for almost two years as his foster care worker until his discharge (aged out) from the child welfare system at age 18.

Client Engagement

Because Dan and I had a prior therapeutic relationship, he talked freely about why he wanted therapy. With most clients, I find it important to establish an environment where people can feel free to share their most intimate thoughts and feelings. As clients begin to find sanctuary in the therapeutic environment, their comfort level increases and they begin the process of establishing a relationship. Central to this concept of sharing is trust. Clients need to believe what you say. They are coming to you because they lack some skill that prevents them from resolving the issue without your assistance. I believe that people are capable of change and want to reach a level of positive equilibrium. They want you to help them achieve that balance. To take the steps necessary for change, they need to trust that you will not abandon them.

I try to establish trust by tailoring engagement to the individual. With some people, I talk about the process of therapy. Some clients want to know why I think I can help them. Still other people want a casual conversation to relax before they discuss their problem. Each person has a different reason for being there and part of my job is to help decide what he or she needs in order to engage in the process. The key to engagement is creating an environment that allows the client to have some control over one aspect of his or her life.

Presenting Problem

None of the engagement techniques was necessary for Dan to engage in the therapeutic process. He started talking as if five years ago were yesterday. Dan said that he was having problems forming relationships with people. His chief reason for coming in for treatment was because he was having difficulty forming "good" relationships with peers, feeling lonely, and not understanding where he fits in terms of his family. He also complained of getting stressed out in relationships. He felt at times that he did not want to put the effort into them because of the stress and feelings of inadequacy by others, especially women. He indicated that at times, it was difficult for him to have fun, and so he retreated to his work.

Questions

The client has presented you with the presenting problem. However, there is some disagreement in the literature about how to proceed. When working with a client, is the presenting problem the actual problem or is it the symptom of an underlying problem? How you would proceed with this case would depend on that answer.

1. Review the literature on the concepts of presenting problem and underlying problem. How is each concept defined and used in treatment?

Based on the information provided so far, please respond to the following questions about this case.

2. What is your hunch about whether the presenting problems are the actual problems?

3. If the presenting problems were the actual problems, how would you proceed with this case?

4. If the presenting problem was the symptom, how would you proceed with this case?

Psychosocial Assessment

When working with clients, I try to conduct a psychosocial assessment. A psychosocial assessment collects information on the biological, physical, social, developmental, emotional, and functional history of the client. The timing of when I gather that information depends on the nature of the presenting problem, and if the client is in crisis. When a client is in crisis, addressing the crisis is my primary concern. Since Dan was not in crisis, I collected the psychosocial information early in the session.

Psychosocial History

Dan, age 23, was born in a small city in the Midwest. He grew up in a small rural town, living in mobile homes. Dan was very small in stature as a child, but grew to 5'10" tall and weighed about 180 pounds. He was in good physical health, took no medications, and had no allergies. He worked as a carpenter's assistant on a full-time basis. Dan was the oldest sibling in a blended Caucasian family of five.

Dan's uncle, who was also his adoptive father, Mr. Ted Kingsley (45 years old), worked as a truck driver. He had a variety of other jobs, including working as a farmer. Dan described Mr. Kingsley as a hard-working man who worked long hours for little money.

Mrs. Kim Kingsley (age 46), Dan's biological mother, suffered from asthma, which limited her physical activity. She was on medication and apparently often had attacks, which at times caused her to see the doctor immediately for a shot or emergency treatment. Mrs. Kingsley worked in the home.

Dan's biological father, Bob Kingsley (age 47), left the family when Dan was an infant and moved in with another woman. He worked in a factory. Dan never had regular contact with his biological father; however, he recently had contact with him at a family member's funeral. Bob did not acknowledge Dan as his son and was distant and aloof.

Approximately a year after Dan's biological father left the family, Dan's mother, Kim, married Bob's brother, Ted. Ted then adopted Dan, and with his wife adopted a second child, Tammy. That marriage ended in divorce four years later when Kim left with another man. Ted obtained custody of Dan and Tammy.

With Kim gone, Ted became the primary caretaker for the children. Ted left Dan and Tammy with various caretakers while he was away driving truck. Ted then married Beth Smith (38 years old), who at that time had two children of her own to care for. Elizabeth and Ben were ages 12 and 14 at the time of the marriage. Ted and Beth then had a child, Christi.

A New Placement for Dan

At age 10, Dan's parents, Ted and Beth, took him to a mental health agency for an assessment because they thought he had severe behavioral problems that they could not control. Dan's parents described him as defiant, lacking emotion, bedwetting, stealing food, sexually experimenting, and possibly abusing his younger sister. His parents reported that Dan had difficulty bonding to others. After an assessment, Dan was placed in a residential program for two years. That was where I first met Dan. While there, Dan received individual and group therapy. One year after Dan's placement in the residential treatment program, Ted divorced Beth after four years of marriage and maintained custody of Dan and Tammy.

The therapy at the residential facility addressed Dan's behavioral and emotional needs. In the individual sessions, Dan talked about his family and the sense of rejection he felt. In the group sessions, the counselor used peer interaction to help children form relationships, learn how other children handled their problems, and hold each other accountable for their own actions. Dan had difficult interacting with the other children in group. He would engage in behaviors that isolated him from the other children. Dan found comfort interacting with the adults at the residential facility, and he stayed away from most of the other children.

During his stay in residential treatment, Dan's biological mother and father never visited him. He had infrequent visits from Ted and Beth. Beth continued to attend the visits with Ted even after the divorce. Dan was slow to talk about his feelings, but they played out whenever he was upset. Although Dan had not suffered abuse and neglect from Ted and Beth, he was always anxious before a visit and exhausted after their visit. When they did not show for a scheduled visit, he exhibited disruptive behaviors and acted out toward the staff and children in the facility.

During the visits with Ted and Beth, there was little physical contact. Ted would shake Dan's hand or pat him on the back. Beth would give him a brief embrace. The rest of the time they would sit around a table while Ted talked about the weather, sports, and cars, and Beth would tell him how the other children were doing. They never talked about Dan going home, how his treatment was progressing, or why their visits were infrequent. After an hour, Ted and Beth would tell Dan it was time for them to leave. They only had brief sessions with the therapist, but never to the point of engagement. They told the therapist that they loved Dan, but they could not provide for his needs. The facility attempted to call Dan's biological parents, but they never responded.

After every visit, Dan went back to his room, laid on the bed, and fell sleep. After sleeping, he would not talk to anyone for the rest of the day. He kept to himself and would read or watch television. In his therapy sessions, he would only say that he was happy to see them and he hoped they would visit.

Therapeutic Foster Care

While Dan was in the residential treatment program, there were concerns about the neglect and possible abuse he received while living with different family members and about the lack of family involvement in treatment. The residential facility referred the case to Children's Protective Services and, after two court hearings, Dan became a temporary ward of the court. That meant that the juvenile court and not his parents were legally responsible for Dan. The foster care worker assigned to the case had several meetings with the staff as they developed long-term treatment options for Dan. At age 12, Dan moved into a therapeutic foster home after the successful completion of the residential treatment program.

A therapeutic foster home is an intensive therapeutic foster care placement. The foster parents, who are part of the foster care team, assist the foster care worker in developing treatment plans, attending court hearings, and providing the extensive supervision that the foster child needs. These placements are primarily two parent foster homes, where the parents receive six weeks of training before placing a child in their home. After the training is complete, the parents must receive ten hours of training per year, and they must participate in a monthly support group with other therapeutic foster parents. The foster parents can have biological children in the home, but the foster child is usually the youngest. This is to ensure that the foster child will not abuse one of the other children in the home. A therapeutic foster home can only have one foster child in the home at a time. Because of the amount of time and energy extended, it is difficult for foster parents to supervise two or more children at the same time. The foster parents are also required to take the children to their numerous counseling or medical appointments. Each foster family is pared with another foster family in order to provide each other peer support, and respite care, as a way to reduce burnout. These supports can assist in reducing the stress on the family and allow them time to function within the struggles of providing twenty-four-hour care.

While Dan was in foster care, additional allegations of abuse and neglect surfaced. After his adoptive father and biological parents refused to participate in any planning for Dan, the foster care worker petitioned the court to have their parental rights terminated. Dan became a permanent ward of the court and eligible for adoption.

Dan lived with the foster parents for six years under a permanent foster home agreement. A permanent foster care agreement allows a teenager to "age out" of the foster care system without being adopted or returning to the biological or legal parents or legal guardians. Dan did not want to be adopted, and so he remained in foster care. The foster parents supported the idea of him staying with them until adulthood, but they did not want to be adoptive parents.

Dan bonded to the foster parents, but continued to have difficulties with lying, stealing, hiding food, and bedwetting up until the time he left their home. Dan reported throughout his extensive involvement with a number of professionals many disturbing details of his childhood and his dealings with those traumas. He resided in the foster home until he completed high school at age 18, and then moved into an apartment. He still had frequent contact with the foster parents and saw them as his family.

Questions

1. Based on the information contained above, construct a genogram that represents Dan's family. What patterns do you see emerging from the genogram? What further information do you need to complete the exercise?

2. The author has provided you with some background information on Dan and his family. From your assessment to this point, discuss if Dan's history relates to his presenting problems.

When children are in long term foster care, the possible outcome is for them to age out of the child welfare system. At age eighteen, Dan did age out, and moved from the foster home to his own apartment.

3. From the professional literature, what types of skills are necessary for children aging out of the foster care system to have in order to live successfully on their own in adulthood?

4. From your review of the literature, you have identified the independent living skills that are necessary for children to have as they move into adulthood. From your assessment of Dan, which of the independent living skills does Dan have? Based on your comparison, discuss if Dan has enough of the independent living skills to function successfully as an adult.

5. Are there programs in your community to assist foster children aging out of the foster care system to function independently? Describe the types of services they provide.

6. From the professional literature, discuss the research on the success of independent living programs.

7. What is your state policy on children who, at a certain age, can refuse to be adopted?

The Psychosocial History Continues

When working with clients, I noticed that some are linear in their thought process. Those clients have a starting point and provide regimented order to their story. Dan liked to move back and forth in time when he talked about his life. Dan remembered at age 2-1/2 his biological mother leaving him in soiled diapers for hours on end. He remembered crying and screaming, wanting her to come and change him, and her not responding to his requests for hours. He identified feelings of abandonment by his mother and indicated that these situations occurred on a regular basis. In fact, they were the normal relational interaction.

Dan described himself as the scapegoat and bad child in the family when he lived with his step-dad (uncle) and mother. His adoptive father severely physically disciplined him for no apparent reason. He recalled his biological mother punishing him physically and emotionally by withholding food for up to two days due to his bedwetting and lying. In order to eat, he would steal food from the pantry in the basement. His mother locked him in the basement, underneath the steps for hours with his bed, due to his bedwetting problem. He indicated that his stepmother would not let him sleep over with the other children in the neighborhood due to his bed-wetting and the urine smell.

As Dan talked about his family, he would move between talking about his biological parents and adoptive parents. He talked about incidents that occurred years apart as if one incident directly followed another incident with no clear gap in time. In addition, during his recounting of events, he presented himself as tranquil with no outward expression of stress or discomfort. Dan appeared to almost enjoy talking about his life experiences.

Dan recalled being sexually abused at a very young age but did not know by whom and exactly how he was abused. He indicated in therapy that he knew something happened that was terrible. He did report experimenting sexually with other boys in the neighborhood at a young age. Dan believed that his sexual behavior extended to him sexually molesting his sister in retaliation against how his stepmother treated him. He indicated he used to fondle his younger sister and threatened to kill the family cat, a close companion of his sister, if she told anyone.

Questions

Dan recalled incidents of sexual abuse at a young age. He is not sure about the age span of the abuse or what type of sexual abuse he experienced. In addition to the abuse, Dan sexually experimented with boys in the neighborhood, fondled his sister by force, and threatened to kill the family cat as a means to get his sister to comply.

1. The concept of repressed memories is controversial. Review the professional literature on whether repressed memories exist.

2. Review the professional literature on sexual abuse. Discuss the findings on adults repressing part or all of the sexual abuse they experienced as a child. Discuss the treatment approaches to assist adults in recovering those repressed memories.

3. How does the professional literature explain why children would sexually abuse other children? Is sexual abuse a learned behavior?

4. Will the majority of children who were sexually abused, sexually abuse other children? How does the professional literature address this topic?

Dan became a Christian while he was in foster care and continued to attend the same Baptist church he attended while living in the foster home. He was involved in youth group activities at the church and school, and he continued his involvement in those activities after high school. Dan found comfort in the teachings of the church but struggled with interacting with people. There was always his fear of doing something inappropriate.

The psychosocial assessment provided information on Dan's life and the challenges he had to face. On some subjects, Dan had a great deal of insight into his problems and seemed to have a high level of understanding as to how these problems affected his functioning. In other areas, Dan was struggling to find the answers that would change his life for the better.

Questions

1. Discuss how religion or spirituality can play an important role in people's lives? What are ways you could introduce religion into the therapy process?

2. If your religious beliefs are different from your clients, explain how that could affect your relationship with the client and your intervention approach.

Theoretical Orientation/Modality

With some of the psychosocial history completed I next turned to theoretical approaches in working with Dan. The theoretical approaches used in this case included eclectic methods incorporating behavioral and psychoanalytic approaches. Dan had been in therapy and treatment for many years, and his problems and challenges were chronic and perpetuated over most of his life. I scrutinized those environmental events, either preceding or following a particular behavior, and used that approach in understanding how his environment affected Dan in adult life.

I discussed how, at his current age, his behavior affected his environment in relationship to how others perceived and dealt with him and what consequences he might have received due to his chosen behavior. An example of those behaviors included bedwetting (since age 6), lying, and stealing. After medical doctors examined him for bed-wetting, they placed him on medication and used an alarm clock. However, that did not decrease his bedwetting. Therefore, how he learned to cope with problems in his youth was manifesting itself in his coping behaviors in adulthood.

The psychoanalytic approach, founded and developed by Sigmund Freud, "postulates the principle of psychic determinism, and believes that everything a person dreams, feels, thinks, fantasizes, and does has a psychological motive" (Strean, 1986, p. 19). That inner unconscious force will motivate Dan in his life decisions such as who he marries, what type of work he does, and how he decides to love and receive love (Binswanger, Boss, & May, 1976; Frank, 1973). "The stages of development in which the child is seen as being 'polymorphously perverse' " (deriving pleasure from bodily activity) are closely looked at as well as the defense mechanism, which the client utilizes" (Strean, 1986, p. 26).

I used those two modalities because of the nature of Dan's multifaceted problems and life experiences. Dan had been in therapy for years, and had chronic and significant problems he needed to deal with. One cannot ignore the vast amount of information about Dan as well as the chronic nature of his complaint. All of that information was included when developing a treatment plan.

Treatment Plan

I had been seeing Dan for six months. The case was in the middle phase of treatment and I anticipated that treatment would conclude in another six months. That timeframe was because of the way Dan processed information before making decisions, a direct response to his lack of impulse control as a child. He felt he had no control over how other people treated him, and he acted out those same responses onto others. Dan thought that people were acting without thinking things through. Therefore, he decided that before he made any decisions, he would process them first. Because therapy was a major decision in his eyes, he processed each session, asked numerous questions, and looked for alternatives to the path he was thinking about taking.

Family Ties

During the sessions, Dan was still visiting with the foster family on a regular basis and saw them as being stable and supportive. He had been attempting to spend time with his biological father, but his father was busy with work. Dan reported that his father has willed all of his personal property, including his house and belongings, to Dan's stepsister. Dan did not appear to be upset that his father helped his stepsister. What upset Dan was that his father would not share of piece of himself with his son.

I have worked with a number of clients, especially teenagers, who had little or no contact with their father. If they found something that belonged to their father, they would beg to have it. I have seen beaten up and tattered baseball gloves, books, magazines, watches, toys or a piece of train track—anything, children could find that would connect them to their father and give them a sense of belonging to a family. Therefore, I could understand why Dan was upset that his father would not give a part of himself.

At first, Dan played down his biological father's apparent lack of interest in spending time with him. He understood that his father needed to make a living, and that not everyone could have flexible jobs. As we talked more about that relationship and what Dan wanted out of it, he began to show some emotion. Dan would say, "If I had a son, I would make time for him." Although Dan is an adult, there was still a part of him that wondered what role he played in his parents' leaving him.

Dan clung to the idea of a positive relationship with his father as he saw with other families. He saw a relationship between the problems in his adult life and the lack of a relationship with his father. Listening to Dan, I had to clarify whether he was talking about his biological, adoptive, or foster father. At times, I was unsure who he was discussing.

As I worked with Dan, I could not help but think about my own family. There were times I wondered what my life would be like if my father had not been there for me. When I thought of my father, it helped me understand how that issue was tearing at Dan. In the end, Dan could never control his father; but, he can decide how to develop and maintain positive relationships with people who want to interact with him.

Questions

The concept of family is not only debated in literature and politics, but people are grapping with that concept in their daily lives. From the legal to the emotional definition of family, people are searching for a sense of belonging.

1. How do you think Dan would define family? What examples in the case support that definition?

2. How does the professional literature define family? As you explore the literature from different professions, does the definition of family change? Discuss the similarities and differences you saw in the definitions of family.

3. Since Dan's foster father has played the role of father in his life, why do you think Dan still has this intense desire to establish a relationship with his biological father?

Working Toward Change

Dan had a tendency to talk about his weaknesses, so I asked him to describe his strengths. Dan thought a long time before answering my question. If I had said to him, "Tell me what's wrong with you," he would not have hesitated to tell me. However, when it came to strengths, Dan struggled to share his positive side. Dan included his strengths as committing himself to social activities, being a hard worker, taking care of his physical self, being loyal to the foster parents, having a good sense of humor, and being able to engage in social activities. He also had been taking therapy seriously and had worked at improving his self-esteem.

I saw his weaknesses as low self-esteem, being unsure of himself, having difficulty forming and maintaining relationships, and acting immaturely. He also found it difficult to express feelings and to trust others. Dan held a lot of anger inside, often cut himself down, and blamed himself as a way of ventilating and projecting his anger.

Dan did not feel worthy to go to certain social activities, explaining that he did not deserve to experience pleasure from that activity. He often sold himself short and was quick to avoid challenges that were well within his ability level. He would stay home and watch television by himself. Defense mechanisms used frequently by Dan included regression, turning against the self, and isolation.

Questions

1. Based on the information contained above, update your genogram on Dan. What changes have occurred since the first genogram? Has your treatment plan changed with the updated information?

2. Develop a list of Dan's strengths.

3. Dan's stated strengths contradicted what he listed as his presenting problems and what the author saw as his weaknesses. In a group, discuss the inconsistencies, and develop an explanation for those inconsistencies.

Goals for Treatment

While working with Dan, we developed a list of goals. I believe that clients must have an endpoint when they start therapy. They should be working toward a goal that would signify the end of therapy. The therapy sessions should also assist the client in seeing if progress is being made. Outside of the therapy sessions, clients should be able to chart their own progress and see how close they are to their end goals. The list below represents what Dan wanted to address.

1. Explore the "realistic" relationship between Dan and his biological family. Discuss how this might be affected by his past and present experiences, and how it might affect his current functioning as well as the relationship with his foster family.
2. Discuss past relationships, current relationships, the components of relationships, and what Dan expects from relationships.
3. Continue to build self-esteem.
4. Increase stress management skills.
5. Develop a healthy balance of work and play activities.

Questions

1. **Based on your assessment of the case, what goals would you have developed for Dan? Review the professional literature to find support for each of your goals. If your goals are the same as Dan's, still find support in the literature for those goals.**

2. **Once you have identified your goals, identify the theoretical model you would use to work on those goals. Select one of your goals and demonstrate how the model works with that goal.**

Treatment

Dan invested in therapy and began addressing the agreed upon goals. He identified areas that he wanted to work on and indicated that he had a real desire to work those things out in order to "make life better" for himself. Dan had been motivated for treatment since the beginning of our relationship.

Six months into the case, we were in the middle phase of treatment and change was slow and difficult for Dan. His resistance to change included his intrapsychic conflict and the confusion he had about his family, especially his present and past relationships with them. He struggled with his allegiances to the foster parents, who were the most consistent and trustworthy adults in his life, and that of his biological parents, who were supposed to have provided a consistent presence in his life. Dan thought that if he got too close to the foster family, he would be seen as rejecting his biological parents. His concept of family was so encompassing that he could not separate the families. That problem manifested itself in the therapy sessions when he would talk about growing up and would jump from family to family as if they were all the same people. Without my previous work with Dan, I would have been unclear if the abuse he experienced occurred in the biological, adoptive, or foster home.

Dan experienced rejection from his biological family and was distrustful and suspicious of their involvement in his life. In therapy, that played out in the fantasies he had about his family being picture perfect, while at the same time seeing the reality in how his family treated him. At times, he put a false sense of hope in his biological family, telling me of dreams he had depicting his family in a positive light. Another time he would explain how cruel, inconsistent and abusive they really were to him. Dan was able to see and verbalize that his family had been dysfunctional, rejecting, and negative toward him in their actions.

Dan did have deficits when it came to his ability to understand his problems and life experiences. He did not know which of his friends to tell about his family, foster care, and residential treatment. It also was difficult for Dan to express emotions, and he often put on a tough exterior in order to cover up his hurting inner self.

I believed that Dan ultimately learned to adapt and cope in such a disorganized and unstable system by becoming unpredictable, oppositional, impulsive, and passive-aggressive. With those learned features in Dan's personality, he was limited in the degree that he could change and revise his present and future functioning. His anger about his family-of-origin issues appeared to be chronic and pervasive, and he would likely carry that into his relationships.

The Next Step

I believed that his intellectual controls and ego defenses had grown, and he did seem to have gained greater control of his impulsivity. Therapy had provided Dan with tools to develop his method of coping with difficulties in life. He had gained a more realistic picture of his family of origin, and had improved his self-esteem to the point where he believed he could do more things personally, socially, and interpersonally. He was able to talk about his family, and his expectations of his family were increasingly more realistic.

Dan had been resistant to discussing sexuality. Due to him experiencing sexual abuse, that issue needed further exploration. Dan minimized that abuse and avoided the discussion of it. I hoped, in the next few months, Dan would discuss his relationships with women, men, and his parents.

Therapeutic Alliance

In each session with Dan, I continued to be supportive of him expressing his feelings and talking about very difficult issues as well as being empathic and letting him know that our sessions were a place for him to feel safe. Roles with Dan included the classical transference role where I represented significant people from his past, including his father, mother, and at times the foster parents. Reflecting from their perspectives had enabled Dan to evaluate the relationship in a more realistic light. Dan was quick to alert me when I reminded him of one of his relatives. When there was transference, most of the time I reminded him of his father; however, it was difficult at times to know which father I was playing in the session.

Dan is an "explorer:" "where he wants an existential alliance and prefers a therapist who is supportive, a knowledgeable co-worker who functions as a guide into his psychological inner space" (Beitman, 1987, p. 54). Often, Dan was asking me for interpretations, thoughts, support, and evaluation of his experiences, feelings, and insights. He needed reflections and reassurances as to what decisions he may make or what emotions he may experience.

Transference

On more than one occasion, Dan had indicated that I had done something that reminded him of his abusive father. One time we were discussing a church activity he had thought about attending. He indicated to me, after becoming a bit hostile, that I used a phrase that his dad frequently used when his parents would argue. That, for Dan, was not pleasant, and he quickly wanted to discuss another issue.

Dan indicated that at times it was very hard for him to get emotionally close to the foster mother during his placement in her home. I believed that the relationship with his mother was so negative and inconsistent that he had difficulty with any female relationship. He never had the chance to form any kind of Oedipal complex or relationship with his mother in his early years because he never had the same mother for very long.

Evaluation of Practice

Dan had benefitted in many ways from the treatment process. He had developed a greater, better ability to discuss the issues in his life instead of acting them out. He had developed his self-esteem. He had improved his ability to express his anger. He also had increased the realistic view of his family. However, all of those issues continued to need work. Dan had experienced a very chronic form of long-term abuse and rejection from his family, with no opportunity to develop a healthy relationship with his mother in the early stages of his developmental life. He carried that inability to form healthy interactions with most of his relationships with females.

Prognosis

Dan had been dependent on the child welfare system for his psychological and physical health due to his family system's dysfunction and disorganization. That, in my opinion, would cause him to be involved with the mental health system at some level throughout his life. Dan would always need a system intervening in his life. The system had been Dan's family, and I believe that he would use it as such, turning to it for the remainder of his life. One can only hope that Dan would be involved on the preventative end rather than the punitive end of the mental health system. It did seem that he had the ability to seek out help when he needed it, and that would be a strength for him in the future.

Dan had completed high school and maintained a job. He had goals of becoming a carpenter, and of someday having a family home. I believed that if Dan utilized services like individual counseling when he felt the need to, he would continue to function productively in society. If Dan did not desire to use the system on a preventative basis, he would experience serious unresolved problems in his life.

I anticipated working with Dan for at least six more months. His prognosis was good as long as he relied on some form of therapy to help him resolve issues as they surfaced in the upcoming developmental stages in his life. Most of his developmental stages were disrupted in one form or another, which would always affect his functioning. We would continue to set goals and work toward Dan living a healthy life.

Questions

Dan has spent most of his life in the child welfare system. His has had a number of primary caretakers, and a number of professionals work with him.

1. Design an intervention plan for Dan. Include in your plan timeframes, intervention model, what you hope to accomplish, and what things would change in his life as an indicator that the goals have been met.

2. Based on this review, what additional or alternative approaches could the author have used with this case? That is, if you were the practitioner, how would you have approached this case? Please explain and justify your approach.

3. Were there any specific interventions or strategies that you disliked or liked? Please explain your opinions.

4. Based on your assessment, discuss whether Dan will need therapy for the rest of his life.

Bibliography _____

Beitman, B. D. (1987). *The structure of individual psychotherapy.* New York: The Guilford Press.
Binswanger, L., Boss, M., & May, R. (1976). Existential therapies: The quest for transcendence. In J. Ehrenwald (ed.), *The history of psychotherapy: From healing magic to encounter* (pp. 371–405). New York: Jason Aronson.
Frank, Jerome D. (1973). *Persuasion and healing: A comparative study of psychotherapy* (rev. ed.). Baltimore: Johns Hopkins University Press.
National Association of Social Workers (2000). *Code of Ethics of the National Association of Social Workers.* Washington, DC: Author.
Strean, H. S. (1986). *Countertransference.* New York: Haworth Press.